Isaiah
41:9b-16

Zephaniah
3:17

THE
CRY OF

COMPASSION

Dave & Cindy, you are two of our beautiful Lord's special ones. May His gracious anointing continue to be upon

John & Esther
Andersen

John O. Anderson

THE
CRY OF
COMPASSION

BRIDGE PUBLISHING
South Plainfield, NJ

The Cry of Compassion by John O. Anderson
ISBN 0-88270-681-0
Library of Congress Catalog Card Number Pending
Copyright © 1994 by John Anderson

Published by:
Bridge Publishing Inc.
2500 Hamilton Blvd.
South Plainfield, NJ 07080

To the memory of

FRED HOFER (1863-1954)

My great-grandfather who was born in Switzerland and emigrated to the United States with his parents. While a young married man he was converted to Christ, and from then on lived joyfully with a heart after God. His spiritual influence on me was immense.

Contents

Foreword

John Anderson's message blows like a crisp, cool wind through the fog of compromise and sloppy thinking that envelopes so much of the contemporary church. The Christians of the West are paying a heavy price for their failure to heed the messages of Israel's prophets. Yet many of these—especially Amos, Hosea, and Jeremiah—confronted a society experiencing moral and spiritual decline that almost exactly mirrors the conditions of the world around us today.

In one decisive respect, however, we have sunk even lower than the people of Israel and Judah in the period of their decline. Many sections of the contemporary Church have joined secular society in endorsing the systematic murder of unborn children through abortion. Often, too, this has been carried out without even the elementary concern that a physician normally exhibits for any patient he is treating.

According to Anderson's estimates, it is possible that as many as one billion babies have been aborted worldwide in the past twenty years. The mass slaughter carried out in Europe during the holocaust in World War II now appears as a pale precursor to the systematic extermination of unborn children that has been practiced all over the world for almost three decades.

Anderson further points out that one main emphasis of the prophets in the Bible is God's special concern for the fatherless, and His avowed commitment to avenge any mistreatment of them. When His judgments finally fall on our corrupt and careless nations, people will surely ask of the professing Christians, and especially those who call themselves *ministers*, "Why didn't you ever warn us?" For Christians to keep silent at a time like this or to remain neutral is, in effect, to renege on their commitment to Christ.

Abortion, however, is only one glaring symptom of a society that has deliberately turned its back on God and that openly flaunts its disobedience to Him and its contempt for Him. Isaiah drew a vivid prophetic picture of our contemporary society:

> The earth is also defiled under its inhabitants,
> Because they have transgressed the laws,
> Changed the ordinance,
> Broken the everlasting covenant.
> Isaiah 24:5 (NKJV)

Isaiah closes with a fearful description of the imminent and cataclysmic judgments of God on such a society. I feel that these judgments are closer at hand than most of us are willing to recognize, and that God may not prove to be so "nice" as many contemporary preachers depict Him.

For my part, as one who has been in full-time Christian ministry for nearly fifty years, I was particularly challenged by chapter 6 of this book on "Well-Established Religion" and chapter 7 on "False Prophets."

In chapter 6, the portrait of Amaziah, the priest of

the "State Church" of Israel's northern kingdom, could be applied to countless preachers who occupy the pulpits of contemporary churches. Nothing would need to be changed except the name of the minister and the location of his parish.

I found chapter 7 on "False Prophets" actually frightening in its implications. Anderson clearly demonstrates from the Scriptures that the deceptive comfort offered by the false prophets to people living in open rebellion against God rendered their hearers incapable of receiving the urgent warnings of the true prophets, who were often in a minority of one.

I was led to search my own conscience. Had I perhaps at times been guilty of a similar distortion of God's truth? Had I succumbed to the temptation to proclaim God's promise of healing and prosperity without offering a biblical definition of "prosperity" or emphasizing the moral and spiritual conditions attached to such promises? For my part, at least, I have decided from now on to lay greater emphasis on holiness than on healing and on faithfulness than on prosperity.

I count it a privilege to write this introduction to *The Cry of Compassion.* But at the same time, I need to add a warning. This is not a book for the timid or careless. Reading it may lead you to make significant changes in your personal attitudes or your priorities—or even to your life-style. It is important, however, to remember one thing—every such change that you make will be for your own eternal good!

Derek Prince

1

Our Defining Time

> "You were the model of perfection, full of wisdom and perfect in beauty.
> "You were in Eden, the garden of God; . . . till wickedness was found in you . . . . you were filled with violence, and you sinned . . . .
> "Your heart became proud on account of your beauty . . . . "[1]

Seeing ourselves through the eyes of others is always good for us—and is often humbling.

A few years ago I was a joint speaker at a pastor's meeting in Australia with a godly, humble minister from an island nation. During one of the meetings, he spoke to the pastors, in his kind manner, about his journeys from his "nation in the third world" to visit the "*Big Brother* nations in the first world." His people, he said, were eager to be like "Big Brother" people in dress, possessions, music, just about everything—so he went to see what Big Brother was like.

He visited America and Australia and saw their great cities. But he said when he looked around them, he was greatly troubled in his spirit by the open sins that he saw, and he tearfully told us of several—among them were the constant violence, the immorality of every kind, and the killing of unborn children.

"In every city that I visited," he said, "I went up to the people of Big Brother and asked them, 'Where are you taking us?'" And they had no answer. So I went back to my own country and told my people, 'Let us be careful in what we are doing in following Big Brother; it doesn't look like he is going in a good way.'" Then he looked at each of us and pleadingly asked, "Where *is* Big Brother taking us?"

His caring, unpretentious words stirred our hearts and forced those of us from the western nations to ask ourselves, "Where *are* we taking him?" Where are we taking the nations who look to us to lead them? Where are we taking ourselves? Do we know? Do we even want to know? Do we even care? Our eyes have become so jaded by the growing evil around us that we may no longer be able to see how far down the path of degeneracy we've gone—nor where we are headed. But one thing is certain, our nations cannot long endure the ongoing corruption that is eating into our moral and spiritual fiber.

A Defining Hour

In January, 1991, President George Bush gave his State of the Union address before the joint session of the United States Congress and said about America's involvement in the Gulf War then in progress, "We stand at a defining hour." By that he meant that the United States was irrevocably involved in a critical watershed event that would define its character and determine its future.

In recent years we have had a myriad of such watershed events—those critical events that mark a change of course, a turning point, for nations and people. Some of these events were so momentous that they had people shaking their heads and saying, "I

2

didn't think I would ever live to see this!" Who would have thought, for example, that we would see the fall of the Berlin Wall and the Iron Curtain? Or the opening of Eastern Europe? Or the disintegration of the Soviet Union? Or that any of us would ever see the Prime Minister of Israel, Yitshak Rabin, shaking hands with the head of the PLO, Yassir Arafat, before an international television audience of millions?

Without question, today there are many pivotal, defining events shaking our world. Every day newspaper headlines grab our attention with reports of new political upheavals and continual social and economic struggles in nation after nation. But the days in which we live, which may well prove to be the worst of times, will not ultimately be defined by the world's political, social, or economical problems—we are at a more crucial crossroad than that.

Today it is our sins that are defining us and that are determining our future and the ultimate judgment we will face. This is a spiritual truth that cannot be questioned or altered. Yet sadly, and to our peril, we are ignoring both our sins and their earthly and eternal consequences.

The moral condition of our world today is the same as it was in the days of Noah and the days of Lot. It was those days that the Lord Jesus used as examples of the social conditions and attitudes that will dominate at the time of His Second Coming. The people in the time of Noah and those in the time of Lot were defined by their sins. God looked upon Noah's generation and saw ". . . how great man's wickedness on the earth had become,"[2] and that ". . . the earth was corrupt . . . and full of violence."[3] And of Lot's society in Sodom, God said it was filled with people who were arrogant, overfed, unconcerned, not caring for the poor and needy—haughty people who ". . . did detestable things before me. Therefore I did away with them as you have seen."[4]

In addition to all their other crimes against God, the inhabitants of Sodom practiced a slimy sin of homosexual perversion that spawned an attempted sexual attack upon two of God's holy angels. By so doing, they gave the sin its name and recorded it forever in the pages of infamy: SODOMY!

Both societies, Noah's and Lot's, perished under God's judgment. Noah's world perished in the Flood; Lot's Sodom perished in a rain of fire and brimstone. Yet visitors to either of those times would probably not have seen that anything was wrong with them, and they certainly wouldn't have found anyone who believed that they were imminently facing God's certain and terrible judgment. Optimistic and pragmatic thinking reigned supreme in their times—even as it does in ours.

Of the days of Lot and the people of Sodom, the Lord Jesus said they were eating, they were drinking, they were buying, they were selling, they were planting, and they were building. But on the day that God took out Lot, the only righteous person in Sodom, "Fire and sulfur rained down from heaven and destroyed them all." And of our times, the Lord Christ of heaven and earth said, "It will be just like this on the day the Son of Man is revealed."[5]

The same immorality and violence that brought God's judgment in the days of Noah and the days of Lot dominated the Old Testament nations of Israel and Judah and the pagan nations around them. AND SO DID THE SAME COMPLACENCY! In spite of all the clear warnings that God gave them through His true prophets, the people continually turned away their ears for the tickling and comfort of the sunny messages preached by the false prophets[6]—and so they kept right on sinning, kept right on with life as usual, kept right on until they were destroyed by God's judgment.

Today we are like the people in Noah's day, corrupt

and violent—perhaps even more than they were, for today we kill millions of unborn children through abortions. And like the people of Sodom, we are arrogant and unconcerned—and we permit detestable things before the Lord, including homosexual immorality. Abortion and homosexual degradation are not our only sins, of course, but they help to define our larger and more widespread violence and immorality— and they are signposts that point to our egotistical pride, self-centeredness, and rebellion against God.

Most dangerous of all, however, is the undeniable fact that we are as complacent as the people were in Noah's day, even as the clouds gathered and the first drops of rain fell, and as the citizens of Sodom were moments before fire and sulfur rained upon them. The false prophets of our day have cunningly diverted our attention from our sins and the clear warnings of the Scriptures to those more pleasing topics that tickle our ears and fill their meetings and their pocketbooks. Because we dance to the tune of our flesh, we ignore the troublesome words of the Bible that warn us that all things today are as they were in those ancient societies upon which God poured out the wrath of His righteous judgment.

America and the western nations are at a defining time in their history. In January, 1994, Charles Colson said, "I think we have five years left." If he is right, it is time that we learned quickly how we are defining ourselves—before we have no time left. To do so, we will start with America, the nation that the world watches—and follows. It is neither wrong nor arrogant to say that, "As American goes, so goes the world." So if we can save America, we can save the world.

America has defined itself in at least six major ways—six ways in which it has recast its Christian character and redetermined its future. This short list is far from exhaustive, but it points unerringly to the

5

moral decline of our nation and the very real danger of God soon bringing judgment upon us. If we ignore the implications of this list, we do so to our own peril.

1. America Is Rejecting Its Vow to God and Is Now Profaning His Name.

Our vow to God is printed on our money: "In God we trust." It is also in our Pledge of Allegiance to the Flag of the United States of America: "One nation under God." And it's on a bronze plaque in the Dirksen Office Building of the U. S. Congress. The Declaration of Independence says we were "endowed by our Creator." Each session of the U. S. Supreme Court opens with the cry, "God save the United States and this Honorable Court." The Library of Congress has a multitude of Scripture verses on display. On the walls of the stairwell within the Washington Monument are inscribed the words, "Holiness to the Lord," and "Search the Scriptures." Engraved at the top of the stairwell is, "Praise the Lord." Abraham Lincoln's "Gettysburg Address" is enshrined on the walls of the Lincoln Memorial, and found in it are these words: "This nation under God." And among Lincoln's speeches engraved on the walls of the Memorial are references to "God," "the Almighty," and "the Bible." Furthermore, when the president-elect is inaugurated, he places his hand on a Bible as he takes the Oath of Office and concludes the oath with the words, "So help me God."

These few examples out of many such uses by our government show the commitment the United States has vowed to God—the many oaths it has made to Him in His name. And God demands the keeping of every vow and oath made to Him. He does not take such things lightly, nor dismiss them at all—so He will eternally hold the government and the people of the United States to their words to Him.

But America is foolishly rejecting its God and its vows. Increasingly we tell Him in words and actions, "We no longer need You—and we will no longer have You rule over us!" We are pushing God away and removing Him from virtually every area of our national life. Every day we perjure ourselves before our God and, without conscience or concern, openly and pridefully reject Him before all who will listen— knowing that today a multitude of American citizens will agree with us. In 1992, the Governor of Mississippi commented that America is "a Christian nation." For this now-unacceptable statement he was violently castigated, some even demanding that he take back and refute his comment. One U.S. senator, theoretically representing the people of his state, said about the comment, "That's deeply offensive to many Americans, frankly, including me."

Our national recognition of God is now a hollow profession, a book-cover facade hiding the pages on which are recorded the hideousness of our national hypocrisy. Our national oath is a lie in the mouth of our country, a blasphemy of which we are increasingly guilty, a violation of God's third commandment: "You shall not take the name of the Lord your God in vain . . . ." To our peril we ignore the warning of that commandment: ". . . For the Lord will not hold him guiltless who takes His name in vain."[7] Such dangerous violations have become so blatant that it is now acceptable for a hypocritical politician, even one who borders on atheism, to conclude a speech with the words, "God bless America."

The prophet Jeremiah, in his address to Judah, prophetically described us: "You [God] are always on their lips but far from their hearts."[8] We are professed believers in God who live as atheists. We are secular citizens of a now ungodly nation—citizens who live AS IF GOD WAS NOT THERE, AS IF HE WAS NOT

7

WAITING FOR US AT HIS JUDGMENT SEAT! If God exists at all, He is now irrelevant to us and to our lives. THIS DEFINES US!

Yet we do not even stop there. To add to the multitude of our sins, we have replaced God with the ultimate idolatry: HUMANISM—a system of thought that centers on human beings and their values, capacities, and worth—a system that makes human beings the center and purpose of their own universe and that has no place in it for God. The human being has become our idol, and in our idolatry we have embraced such evil agendas as the "right" to kill an unborn baby—who for the sake of our conscience is now called a "fetus" to make it something not yet human; and the "right" to commit all sorts of sexual perversions—now called "alternate life-styles" for the sake of that same now-overburdened conscience. The sprinkling of the blood of Christ is no longer the cleanser of our conscience,[9] it is now our ability to rename those things that bother us.

But all our foolish twisting of words and our secular posturing mean nothing to God—He is holding us to our oaths and demanding that we keep our vows.

If we continue to profess allegiance to God, yet presumptuously ignore Him and reject His standards, He will surely remove His grace from us. America was founded on high ideals and respect for God, but if we say to Him, "God, we do not want You," He will leave us—and may never return. We would then do well to remove from our money the words, "In God we trust," and have printed in their place, "Ichabod . . . The glory has departed."[10] This will be our judgment in this world and in the next—and it is already beginning to happen.

2. America Is Sinning Boldly by Calling Evil Good.

When Alistair Cooke, the British-born American journalist and broadcaster, was asked about Chesterton's famous remark that the United States was a nation with the soul of a church, he replied, "That's true, but also the soul of a whorehouse."[11] Because of its split personality, America has lost its sense of sin and is under the indictment of the prophetic words of the prophet Isaiah: "Woe to those who call evil good and good evil . . . ."[12] The consequence of throwing God out of our nation is to bring our nation under the judgment of His words.[13]

Having rejected God, we grow increasingly devoid of His spiritual values and scriptural principles, and plunge deeper into the dark abyss of self-determination of our moral values. We are no longer a nation that believes in the importance of moral absolutes. America—and the West—has so turned traditional and scriptural moral standards upside down that they are now looked at in two defining ways: 1. AS BEING MORALLY NEUTRAL , and 2. EVEN AS VIRTUES.

In today's twisted spiritual philosophy, sins that involve sexual immorality and abortion are relegated to the ethical middle-ground—a foggy, gray area that lies somewhere between right and wrong, and where doing whatever is right in your own eyes is canonized. In that shrouded area you are free to commit abortion, to fornicate, to practice homosexual perversions— whatever you choose to do in whatever way you choose to do it. Gray is in, moral judgments are out, right or wrong no longer exist, and whoever calls sin "sin" is quickly and automatically castigated. Americans have become as the Lord said of Israel, "They do not know how to do right," and as Isaiah wrote, "We have turned, every one, to his own way." There are no better definitions of our nation's moral climate than those.

Sexual immorality and the slaughter of unborn babies are now virtues in the eyes of many—good things to do if pleasurable or expedient. Once marriage between heterosexual partners was the only one acceptable—indeed, the only one thought of by anyone. But now the coupling of immoral partners—unmarried men and women, or homosexuals, living together—is equated with traditional marriage, and in many states is now legally equivalent. Many evils are now called "good."

God created us male and female, men and women—we are one or the other. He did not create a third sex—there is no "it" in the Bible's record of creation. Yet our immoral society has elevated homosexuality to the status of a third sex—and our tax-funded public schools are teaching our God-given children that they have three choices of sex orientation, and they can choose to be whichever one they feel is right for them. Evil is called "good."

Our worst crime, however, is abortion. Its rationale is that it's "a woman's right to do with her body whatever she wants to do." To many, this "right" has become like the constitutional right of free speech, of religion, of the press—it is inviolable, a right that cannot be taken away. But this argument is ludicrous. None of us, not even women, have the right to do whatever we want to do with our bodies—both suicide and the use of drugs are illegal. And the woman who has an abortion is not destroying her body, she is destroying the body of the baby in her womb. Evil is called "good."

Many concerned people view abortion as "a compassionate action." The compassionate concern, of course, is always for the pregnant woman, not for the baby. The woman's dilemma may be that she's unmarried, or already has what she feels are too many children, or believes that having a baby will hurt her career—or her figure, or both. There is also the unbelievable rationale that if the baby is allowed to be born it might have a "bad life." It might, for example, be an unwanted child, be born of abusive parents, be born into poverty, or be born handicapped—and in today's society, any of these are considered justifiable reasons for aborting the child. Killing the unborn has become a compassionate action in the minds and hearts of many. Great evil is called "great good."

America has given birth to these justifications for killing the unborn child in the womb, and she has further turned reason and justice upside down by proclaiming that to deny a woman the "right to abortion" is what is really evil and wrong. Good is called "evil."

Abortion defines us.

3. America Is Officially Permitting the Shedding of Innocent Blood.

We'll look at this in more detail later, but we must understand that we have the blood of a multitude of unborn innocents on our collective hands—and each of us will give account to God for our part in this national holocaust. The implications to us are enormously grave. America is committing "crying sins" as the blood of millions of slain unborn children cries out to God for vengeance—just as did the blood of Abel.[14] America and the nations of the West now have one of the things that God hates: "Hands that shed innocent blood."[15] The "cry of the innocents" defines us.

4. America Has Created a "Fatherless Generation."

This defining reality we will also look at in greater detail later, but it is tightly interwoven with number three. America has an epidemic of fatherlessness. An unprecedented multitude of errant men are leaving their children—born and unborn—without care or protection.

Perhaps the fastest growing group in America today

is single-parent families—most of them in the ghettos and most of them headed by women. A significant and growing segment of our society is growing up without a father.

But most damning is the fact that we have now legally declared that an unborn child in America cannot be protected by his or her father. Thus, in a very real sense, every unborn child is fatherless.

The seriousness of fatherlessness is staggering—it points with tiny but unerring fingers to God's judgment that we so rightly deserve—and will so soon receive. Those tiny fingers alone should put every father on his face in repentance before the heavenly Father who loves and will protect the fatherless.

The defining cry of every child of this generation is, "Where is my father?"

5. America Is Living as if Choices Do Not Have Consequences.

God's Word is clear and certain—what we sow is what we reap, and the wages of sin is death. Yet we live as if we can sin without reaping the consequences. Like the woman in the Garden of Eden, we believe the serpent's lie, "You will not surely die."[16] The prophet Zephaniah could easily have been writing about us when he wrote about those who were saying, "The Lord will do nothing, either good or bad."[17] Today we sin brazenly without concern, the blood of destroyed children covers our hands, we openly allow every perverse kind of sexual evil—we have become proud and self-sufficient, independent of the God who created us, and openly reviling Him by saying to ourselves, "He won't call us to account for our sins." Living in denial, we ignore God's certain punitive justice that will come upon us.

Thus the present hour is a pivotal one—we are

under judgment, we are being warned, but we are ignoring both. Instead of responding with repentance, we casually continue to sin, unconcerned that God requires us to answer to Him for the consequences of our sins. With fragile foolishness we ignore the demands of God and clutch precariously onto the disintegrating thread of human effort to save us— something no human being has ever managed to do.

God is not an unconcerned spectator who watches our sins and ignores them. Why are we so presumptuous as to think He does? Do we think we're so great that we can do anything we want to do and a holy and just God can do nothing about it? No country or empire is so strong that it can shake its fist in the face of a righteous God with impunity. The Scriptures and history are littered with the debris of once-powerful nations who permitted moral and spiritual decay to bring them to ruin.

The costs of our sinful choices are already evident. The bills are coming in.

> •One in every 3.5 pregnancies is aborted. So 1.5 million unborn children are killed each year in the United States alone. Fifty million are murdered worldwide each year. With a whole industry specializing in abortion, our land is polluted by innocent blood.

> •One in two marriages ends in divorce.

> •Sexual permissiveness has resulted in increasingly perverted behaviors.

> •Pornography has become a multi-billion-dollar industry.

> •Homosexuality is accepted as a third sex.

• AIDS, and other sexually transmitted diseases, are epidemic—and are raging now even through innocent victims.

• Fifteen million children come home each day to only one parent.

• Drug addiction is out of control, and it has been described as "the war we won't win."

• Enormous pressure is building toward euthanasia for the elderly and the terminally ill, and infanticide against unwanted children.

• Crimes of violence are so rampant that it is unsafe to walk the streets at night in the capital of the United States and in virtually all major cities—and recent reports show that this is becoming true even in our smaller cities and towns.

• The atmosphere of violence is increasing to such an extent that every woman now faces the real prospect of being assaulted, raped, or beaten during her lifetime.

• Over 100,000 guns are now carried to school each day.

• One of the most devastating social revolutions in this generation is militant feminism, a movement which demands the alleged right to kill the unborn, and advocates the right of women to fornicate freely and live whatever sexual life-style they prefer.

•Suicide now ranks as the second leading cause of death among teenagers—just behind car accidents.

•Our national debt is in the trillions of dollars—and is still growing, unaffected by any so-called "deficit reduction" efforts.

These are enormous burdens for us to carry. We are dying the death of a thousand self-inflicted wounds. But each wound reveals how immoral, insensitive, and violent our God-ignoring philosophy is. Those who have preached this godless philosophy are responsible for today's social and moral wreckage and will answer to God for it. But we disregard that fact and live only in the "now." Futurist Watts Wacker says Americans have embraced the motto, "Life is uncertain, eat dessert first."[18] We are as Isaiah said of Judah, who would not admit the idolatrous lies they believed, "He feeds on ashes, a deluded heart misleads him; he cannot save himself, or say, 'Is not this thing in my right hand a lie?'"[19]

America, Canada, Australia, and New Zealand are still young nations that were carved out of virgin lands that were filled with abundant natural resources. We pioneered robust political systems and democratic governments. We worked to build our society, to create an impressive civilization, but we've forgotten that our natural and social gifts came from God. Without God, all our national achievements mean nothing—they are foolish. During our high materialistic ride, we in America and the West lived well for the most part, but the party is over and we are now being called by God to give an account of our stewardship.

In that accounting, we must weigh the question of how is it possible that in no more than two centuries this beautiful land of America has become a sewer of sin, violence, and immorality—and is laden with debt?

Pagan Babylon built a magnificent city and empire, but it ignored God and sinned with abandon. Therefore, God said Babylon would be destroyed. All Babylon's striving to build its empire was futile, "The peoples exhaust themselves for nothing, the nations' labor is only fuel for the flames."[20] So Babylon fell.

When Alexander Solzhenitsyn—after his years in Soviet concentration camps—was allowed to leave Russia and live in the West, he expected to find a strong alternative to God-denying communism. Instead, he found a crisis of the human spirit in the form of materialism, hedonism, and self-indulgence. When he received the "Templeton Prize in Religion" in London, England, Solzhenitsyn said, "Through decades of gradual erosion, the meaning of life in the West has ceased to be seen as anything more lofty than the 'pursuit of happiness.' The concepts of good and evil have been ridiculed for several centuries. It has become embarrassing to appeal to eternal concepts. The West is ineluctably slipping toward the abyss. Losing more and more of [its] religious essence as [it] thoughtlessly yields up [its] younger generation to atheism."[21]

Succinctly, football coach Sam Wyche said, "I don't know but that our country is going to hell in a hand basket and we don't know it."[22]

6. America Has a Distracted Church

The Church in America and in the nations of the West *must* repent. The American Church has enjoyed great blessings from God. Throughout our history it has seen Him move in tremendous spiritual awakenings, and He has enabled it to support great missionary endeavors and ministries. For this we rejoice. But we have been diverted from the spiritual pursuits which have brought such blessings and have become preoccupied with worldliness, doctrinal fads, personal success, pop-psychology, church size, and internal arguments. All this is taking place while godless forces are setting the national agenda; while once-unthinkable sins are openly practiced and accepted; while the nation is increasingly wallowing in evil, violence, crime, abortion, immorality, drugs, AIDS, gang wars, idolatry, humanism, ad nauseam.

Unbelievably, and to our shame, in the face of America's ongoing great sin and its certain judgment, many in the Church have joined the nation in its frolic. God intends us to be prophetic against the sin of our country. Instead, we seek prosperity and continue to squander our spiritual blessings on self-serving doctrines and emphasis. The scandal of our travesty is enormous.

The tragic consequence is that the Church has given our nation the idea that it can sin with impunity. We have allowed people to believe that choices do not have consequences. But God is now holding us accountable and He is speaking strongly to His Church. Too often our message has been watered down to, "God loves you just as you are," and has stopped there. The Scriptures, however, emphasize that God *does* love you, but He also commands you to repent and turn from your wicked ways so that you can have *His* abundant life. The first word of the true Gospel is "Repent."[23]

America is in a moral and spiritual free-fall into a dark pit. Sadly, there is little warning from the Church, because the voice of the Church has been effectively silenced by a feel-good gospel and seduced by self-improvement, success, self-image, and prosperity movements and other distractions. America is like the professional window cleaner who belonged to a self-esteeming, positive-possibility-thinking, optimistic church. One summer day while cleaning windows on the twenty-first floor of an old building, his platform broke loose and he fell. All the windows in the offices were open that day, and as he plummeted down past each window, the people inside could hear him cheerfully confess to himself, "So far, so good! So far, so good!"

Jesus' sharp warning about the complacent, business-as-usual attitude in the times of Noah and the times of Lot was to His Church—He was speaking to us! Our Lord Jesus intended that His Church preach the Word of God, live for eternity as citizens of heaven, take up His cross, and become His powerful voice confronting the immorality of the world's values while calling for repentance. Our age loves the smooth lies of the New Age movement; it loves Eastern religion; and it particularly loves our self-serving, compromising, and distracted Christianity. With these, our nation can sin with abandon without bothering its conscience.

There are over fifty million people in the United States who profess to be born again. That is one out of every five Americans. Impressive figures. Few other countries can boast such statistics. As the light of the world,[24] the brightness of that many Christians should easily be seen. But is it? Is our light shining into the darkness of our nation? Is the brightness of our light showing by contrast how dark our nation's darkness is? Is our light illuminating the pathway to the true Light, Jesus Christ, our Lord? Or have we been seduced by today's paganism and have we put our light under a secularized basket so that we can accommodate the world instead of confronting it? Has the message of the Church become a worldly echo instead of a holy voice?

Richard Halverson, Chaplain of the United States Senate, said, "We [the Church] are badly infected with secularism, with the materialism that says 'live for the now.'"[25] And even the Roman Catholic Pope John Paul said, "The temptation today is to reduce Christianity to merely human wisdom, a pseudoscience of well-being.

In our heavily secularized world a 'gradual sec-
ularization of salvation' has taken place . . . . "[26]

Where is our heart that should be panting after
God?[27] Where is our passion to please only Him? If
we are headed to judgment, why are not we Christians
rushing into the streets urging—even demanding—
repentance and righteousness? Is it because we have,
in fact, taken upon ourselves the attitudes that were
characteristic of the people in Noah's day and in Lot's
day?

Judgment begins at the house of God. So repentance must start in the Church—in us. But what will it
take to stir us—to stir the Church, to stir the world?
What will awaken us to our defining hour? Will it
require additional crises? Economic collapse? More
wars? There have been two major crises in recent years
that should have been wake-up calls: the October, 1987,
stock market crash and the 1991 Gulf War. Both should
have been warnings to decadent America and other
western nations. Both should have shaken us enough
to make us cry out to God in repentance—but both did
not, which is a measure of how hard our hearts have
become. In addition, there has been a sequence of
increasingly severe natural disasters—earthquakes,
fires, floods, tornadoes, hurricanes, volcanic eruptions—and even more severe ones are expected in the
near future. (Read the fourth chapter of the Book of
Amos.)

But we usually fail to discern the signs of the times.
We are like those to whom the Lord Jesus was speaking
when He said, "You know how to interpret the
appearance of the sky, but you cannot interpret [discern]
the signs of the times."[28] When the stock market
crashed, some prayed for God to spare us from
economic ruin. A few days after Iraq invaded Kuwait,
I recall hearing a sincere pastor pray, "Lord, spare us
from war." I was then jarred by a stabbing thought, as

if the Lord was saying, "Spare you? Spare you for what? Spare you so you can continue your self-centered lives? Spare you so you can go right on killing your unborn children whose blood cries for vengeance? Spare you to continue to practice the sins that spread the plague of AIDS? Spare you to continue destroying your families? No, if you are spared, it will be for more than that."

The threat of imminent danger always grabs our attention. Having a hangman's noose around your neck gets your attention every time. However, when the stock market crashed and the Gulf War began, did we focus on the lessons of those events, lessons that should have reminded us that financial and military stability and security can be very tenuous and fleeting? We should have come away from those crises impressed once more by the mercy of God—a mercy given, as always, so we would repent. Repentance is always God's number-one call, and always our number-one need.

But when the crises were over, did we repent and turn to God? No, we praised our financial know-how, our superior technology, and the brilliance and courage of our military and political leaders. Then to our peril, we settled back down again, both the world and the Church, back to life as before—buying, selling, building, planting. The lessons of those events were lost. Because we have rejected God and are sinning so boldly, we are no longer controlling those events that radically affect us, but are simply lurching from crisis to crisis.

We can be certain, however, that other watershed crises on the magnitude of the stock market crash and the Gulf War loom on the horizon ahead of us. Until now we have tended to face our crises in sequence, but that could well change. It is a very real prospect for us that the ravages of our sinful choices will increasingly wreak their bitter consequences on us, leading to multiple crises happening at once in rapid-fire succession: crime, violence, drug addiction, rapidly increasing costs for diseases like AIDS, another war, another stock market crash, a pressing international emergency, inner-city riots, a sudden explosion in our national debt, devastating fires, etc. To these add the staggering financial costs and potential loss of lives caused by natural disasters such as earthquakes, floods, hurricanes, tornadoes, blizzards, volcanic eruptions. If several of these man-made and natural disasters happen at the same time, the toll on us would be enormous. Do we honestly think we could cope with such widespread disaster? Remember, America is a *papier-mâché* society that maintains the image of prosperity by borrowing approximately one billion dollars a day.

We are at a defining time when it will take something more to save our nation than just another election, or spending another chunk of money, or getting things politically correct, or planting more trees, or preserving some endangered species. Our problems are spiritual and that is where we must start. We have a moral sickness, and only repentance will cure us. But we are running out of time.

The great prophet Jeremiah saw the Jerusalem of his day live as if God was not there. He saw compromise and idolatry mixed with the worship of God. He witnessed the people being deluded into believing that God would not judge them, and he saw his beloved Jerusalem running out of time—the destruction of the unrepentant city was fast approaching. He stood as a priest before God and saw His heart and wept. Then he stood before the people as a prophet and proclaimed that their only hope was to be found in God.[29] Jeremiah spoke God's Word resolutely. It burned within him like a cleansing fire, giving no quarter to sin and false prophets.

But tragically for Jerusalem, they paid no attention

21

to Jeremiah. They listened instead to the false prophets, continued in sin, and refused to repent. Jerusalem crossed an invisible moral line, and God judged them. In the same way, God judged the pagan nations.

In his opening prayer at the January 20, 1993, presidential inauguration, Evangelist Billy Graham perceptively prayed, "But we cannot say that we are a righteous people, for we are not. WE HAVE SINNED AGAINST YOU. We have sown to the wind and are now reaping the whirlwind of crime, drug abuse, racism, immorality, and social injustice. We need to repent of our sins and turn by faith to you." Mr. Graham discerningly defined how God now sees our nation.

Contrasting with Mr. Graham's prayer was the political rhetoric of all the political parties in the election campaign leading up to that inauguration. They focused on "buying, selling, building, planting"—business as usual. And it was to the shame of our nation that in his very first days in office, our new president's first actions reflected the immoral direction he was taking the nation—a direction that was contrary to all the Christian words and Scripture verses that he quoted prior to his election. Among the first executive orders that he signed were ones to advance abortion and to put gays into the military—both orders flew directly into the face of Mr. Graham's prayer.

It is now obvious and sad that Billy Graham's perceptive prayer was used by the politicians as nothing more than window-dressing for the new president's inauguration. The moment the inauguration was over, the prayer was gone and forgotten, buried among the inauguration rubble, ignored and unheeded. Each of us, however, needs to look into a mirror of our own, for in the spirit of our times we have all ignored and not heeded the implications of Rev. Graham's prayer.

Has America gone too far? Has America crossed that invisible moral line of no return? Some believe that America has indeed crossed such a boundary, that America has willfully moved itself not only to a post-Christian era, but to a POST-REPENTANCE era. These people believe that America COULD have repented, but now simply WON'T repent. If so, America has rejected God, hardened itself in its sin, and will never turn to the Lord. Is this true? Just having to consider such a question today should shake us, for less than a hundred years ago no one would have ever thought of asking such a question about this Christian nation that ruled itself so proudly and gladly under the rule of God.

Almighty God is just, and He does not wink at sin. Thomas Jefferson said, "Indeed I tremble for my country when I reflect that God is just, and that His justice cannot sleep forever." We must know that while we continue to spend our coins of grace with sinful abandon, we are under indictment: "Because of your stubbornness and your unrepentant heart, you are storing up wrath against yourself for the day of God's wrath . . . ."[30]

We *must* understand that if we reject God, there is no hope for America and, therefore, no hope for any country in the West.

We might not want to believe that America has crossed the moral line of no return, but what is undeniable is that every day in which *America does not repent* only confirms our refusal to do so and only increases our condemnation—and THAT moral line indisputably hastens our judgment.

Perhaps we all need to look into God's mirror and see ourselves as *He* sees us.[31]

---

[1]Ezekiel 28:12b-13a, 15b, 16b, 17a.
[2]Genesis 6:5.
[3]Genesis 6:11.

6666666 66666666 66666666 66666666

66 6666 66666 6666 6666 6666

66 6666 6666 6666 66666 666666 666666 6666 66

66 66 6666666 66 66 66 66 66 66 66 66 66 66

(stop)

[4]Ezekiel 16:49-50.
[5]Luke 17:28-30.
[6]2 Timothy 4:3-4.
[7]Exodus 20:7 (NKJV).
[8]Jeremiah 12:2.
[9]Hebrews 9:14, 10:22.
[10]1 Samuel 4:21.
[11]*Idols for Destruction,* Herbert Schlossberg, (Thomas Nelson Publishers, Nashville, TN). p. 268.
[12]Isaiah 5:20.
[13]John 12:48.
[14]Genesis 4:10.
[15]Proverbs 6:17.
[16]Genesis 3:4.
[17]Zephaniah 1:12.
[18]Watts Wacker, quoted in *USA Today,* October 16, 1991.
[19]Isaiah 44:20.
[20]Jeremiah 51:58.
[21]From "Serving False Gods," by Carl Horn, in *ALL About Issues* magazine, Stafford, VA, March-April, 1987.
[22]Sam Wyche, *The Missoulian,* Missoula, MT, January 23, 1989.
[23]Acts 2:38.
[24]Matthew 5:14.
[25]Richard Halverson, interview in *Christianity Today,* November 12, 1982.
[26]Pope John Paul, "Redemptoris Missio," in *L'Osservatora Romano,* January 28, 1991, p. 6.
[27]Psalm 42:1.
[28]Matthew 16:3.
[29]Jeremiah 9:1, 13:17, 14:17.
[30]Romans 2:5.
[31]James 1:23-24.

2

A Distant Mirror

The ready acceptance of secularism within the Church has had one very important . . . consequence. The more the Church becomes simply a mirror for the values of society, the more marginal it becomes.

John Fleming[1]

Abortion, extramarital affairs, suicide, euthanasia, and homosexuality are now private matters, not Church business.

(From a survey reporting European attitudes.)

Historical moments have often been used to draw parallels with modern society in order to derive lessons for today. Insight from history is desperately needed now, for there is a growing feeling among many people that the foundations of our society are beginning to slide beneath our feet— like some great moral fault-line that is about to give way and create a social-quake that will result in unprecedented disaster. People are beginning to sense that something deep within the nature of our nation is amiss. They are uncertain as to where we are now and fearful of where we are going.

Some of the answers we seek from history can be found in the time of the prophet Amos (about 762 B.C.)—in the conditions he encountered in the Northern Kingdom of Israel and the surrounding pagan nations. George Adam Smith said, "With Amos we stand among the conditions of our day."[2] Amos is a mirror into which we can look and see ourselves as we are today, and see our potential future.

By most economic and political measurements, Amos's era was a successful and secure time. There was peace in Israel, there was prosperity, and prosperity then—as now—was seen as one of God's blessings. So religion flourished.

Israel's situation was similar to Charles Dickens's statement in the opening lines of *A Tale of Two Cities:* "It was the best of times, it was the worst of times." There was great wealth, there was great sin. Israel was a nation that had known God, that belonged to Him, but had rejected Him. The good times flourished—and so did injustice, pride, idolatry, immorality, violence. Sin defined the nation. It was the time of the Northern Kingdom's golden age and its last age—the prosperous nation was headed for judgment and destruction.

Israel's situation was critical. Looming ahead—though they did not know it—was the ominous date of 722 B.C., the year when the unrepentant nation, after many warnings from God's prophet, would fall brutally to the Assyrians under God's judgment. This meant that Israel had about forty years left—from 762 B.C. to 722 B.C.—just forty years. In the rise and fall of nations, especially a nation like Israel that could trace its ancestry back a thousand years to Abraham, forty years was a very short time.

God used Amos to warn and entreat Israel, and to proclaim judgment on the surrounding godless nations. But prosperity had blinded Israel—as it often does both individuals and nations—and she repeatedly spurned God's message, rejected and threatened Amos, and went about business as usual.

To get Israel's attention, God had Amos begin his preaching with fierce words, fiery words, thundering words: "The Lord roars from Zion. . . ."[3] This image of God as an angry lion about to pounce on its prey was meant to jolt Israel and wake her up. The nation's peril demanded boldness and noise from the prophet—so the Lord roared and thundered through Amos.

The Lord's roar at His people, His chosen nation, staggers us—but it was motivated by love for them. They were in imminent peril and He was warning them of their danger. Love roars when it sees a loved one in danger. God had chosen Israel out of all the peoples of the world, and as rebellious as they were, He still loved them. And because He loved them, He would chasten and punish them for their sins that they might return to Him.[4]

> You only have I known of all the families of the earth; therefore I will punish you for all your iniquities.[5]

Israel had known God and His Word, but now they were a nation that no longer knew right from wrong—their spiritual vision had blurred and they could no longer see clearly the ways of God. They had become a nation that did "not know how to do right."[6] They had become an amoral society. They had adopted the values and life-styles of the surrounding pagan nations, and had mixed them in with the moral and spiritual teachings of God. These mixed teachings seared their consciences and dulled the edge of the sword that is the Word of God. And a seared conscience that can no longer discern the things of God easily permits those ungodly things that had once been considered abominations.

Esteemed Australian columnist A. B. Santamaria said, "In the *Brothers Karamazov*, Dostoevsky has his character Ivan say that if immortality (ultimately inconceivable without God) is an illusion, then everything is permissible, even cannibalism."

Israel was indifferent to its danger. "Disaster will not overtake or meet us," they said.[7] They thought they could sin with impunity. But then came Amos who upended their false confidence and accused them of being corrupt and guilty, rebellious sinners who needed to repent. He bluntly told them that they were not the smooth, fashionable people they saw themselves to be, nor were they getting away with their sins as they thought they were. A displeased God was watching them: "Surely the eyes of the Sovereign Lord are on the sinful kingdom. I will destroy it."[8]

Amos was a needed prophetic voice. He was a prophet who proclaimed the clear Word of God to Israel with a stern but caring rebuke, a rebuke intended to open the blind eyes of Israel so it could see its sins and return to its God. We can learn much about ourselves from Amos's message to Israel, and from the eight powerful pronouncements of judgment that he proclaimed against Israel, Judah, and the six surrounding pagan nations.

It is important to us that we examine the pattern of the first six judgments—these concerned Damascus (Syria), Gaza (Philistia), Tyre (Phoenicia), Edom, Ammon, and Moab. Each judgment contains five identical statements. As we examine these statements, pay particular attention to number four; it is this one that we will use to ask a question about ourselves.

1. "THIS IS WHAT THE LORD SAYS." Almighty God is speaking. Each nation is accountable to God, and He is evaluating each one.

2. "FOR THREE SINS . . . AND FOR FOUR. . . ."
This means extensive, habitual sins—committing
one sin after another, creating national guilt.

3. "I WILL NOT TURN BACK MY WRATH."
There would be no mercy. They had to face God's
judgment.

4. "BECAUSE . . . (God names one sin that
particular nation is committing)." This is strategic
and instructive, and we will look at it later in more
detail.

5. "I WILL SEND FIRE. . . ." This describes God's
judgment.

These six nations thought they could get by with sin,
that because they had nothing to do with God, God had
nothing to do with them. They were wrong on both
counts. Look around, where are those six nations today?
Gone! Where are the other nations, like Assyria and
Babylon, or the Greek and Roman Empires, or Nazi
Germany? Also gone!

Now, let's look closer at statement four. God says
each nation had many sins, but He names only one sin
for each. Only one. That has *great* significance for us.
So let's gravely consider what this is saying to us today.

SYRIA: "Because she threshed Gilead with sledges
having iron teeth." The sledge was a heavy wooden
farm instrument, studded underneath with iron spikes.
Oxen pulled it across harvested grain to release the
kernels. Syria had pillaged Gilead, then dragged the
sledge across the people to kill or punish them.

PHILISTIA: "Because she took captive whole
communities and sold them to Edom." The Philistines
were slave traders. They would round up a whole
population, like so many wild horses, and sell them as
slaves to Edom.

PHOENICIA: "Because she sold whole communities of captives to Edom, disregarding a treaty of brotherhood." The Phoenicians also were brutal slave traders who sold people to Edom. But more damning, THEY DID IT AGAINST A BONDED COMMITMENT, just to make money.

EDOM: "Because he pursued his brother with a sword, stifling all compassion, because his anger raged continually and his fury flamed unchecked." Here the "brother" was probably Israel, and Edom put aside brotherly love and continuously treated Israel angrily and murderously. Edom allowed resentment and unforgiveness to rage unchecked.

AMMON: "Because he ripped open the pregnant women of Gilead in order to extend his borders." The Ammonites committed the unspeakable barbaric acts of disemboweling pregnant women. To decrease the future population of Gilead and thereby extend their own borders, the Ammonites tore open the wombs of the pregnant women so that they could destroy their unborn children. Of this barbarism, Francis Foulkes wrote that the Ammonites "dealt savagely . . . they no longer cared about human life nor did they worry about the suffering they caused."[9]

MOAB: "Because he burned, as if to lime, the bones of Edom's king." George Adam Smith said, "To destroy a man's bones was to pursue him even beyond death and condemn his spirit to an eternity of 'homeless wandering.'"[10] So to treat a king's dead body in such a way was an enormous sacrilege, and showed the great callousness of Moab. Moab burned the bones of Edom's king to add to the pain, insult, and abuse of Edom. The act was cruelty against the living, not against the dead.

Those were the sins, all seeming to be somewhat different. However, did you notice the common element in all of them? Different sins, but one element—INHUMANITY. Crimes against humanity, crimes even pagans considered to be wrong. Every sin God named involved some kind of cruelty, brutalization, violence against human life—and each of those sins was permitted by the nation, so each was a national sin.

God used the sin of inhumanity to define each nation. He used it to reveal the nation's larger rampant iniquity. The inhumanity exposed the corrupted nature of the country's character; it defined the level of the nation's degeneracy. That one sin, by itself, showed how great the nation's wickedness had become. The inhumane actions of these six nations revealed a common national character that was so foul it evoked the wrath of God upon each of them. It was if God had said, "Ammon, you are so callous and shameless in your sin that your debased character now condones brutally ripping open the wombs of women so you can destroy their unborn children—therefore, you are judged, and condemned." In the same way, God was saying, "Phoenicia and Philistia, you have become so base that without qualm you raid entire populations and sell them as slaves—therefore, you are judged, and condemned." And He was saying similar things about the other nations. These six nations had each filled their cups of iniquity to overflowing—and God emptied their cups.

Degeneracy doesn't happen overnight. Always there is a gradual searing of the national conscience. In the early stages, the nation's conscience is appalled at heinous evils. But then destructive philosophies slither in and moral values are attacked. People begin to change their thinking, and soon their consciences begin to find room for increasing evil—usually justified in the name of social progress and national good. Soon the day arrives when the unthinkable becomes thinkable, when the unacceptable becomes acceptable, when evil becomes good and good becomes evil.

That is how Nazi Germany came into being. At the turn of this century, no German would have believed that his or her nation would someday slaughter six-million innocent and helpless Jews. Yet it happened. Nazi Germany is now defined by one sin: GENOCIDE.

God's judgment on the nations in Amos's day can encourage us by knowing that our God always deals with injustice—in His own time and His own way. But such knowledge can also frighten us when we think of our own nation. God judged the brutal crimes of Ammon, the slave trading of the Philistines and the Phoenicians, and the brutality of the other nations. They sowed violence, they reaped violence. Choices always have consequences.

But what about our nation? Edom did not get away with its sins, neither did Ammon, nor Syria, nor Moab, nor the Philistines. Neither did Nazi Germany nor the Soviet Union. Why do we think we will get away with our sins? Do we think we are better than they were, more in the favor of God than they were? God does not show partiality to people—or to nations.[11]

Now here is the question that we must ask ourselves: If God were to select one sin today to define our nation, WHAT SIN WOULD HE SELECT? If God, using the prophet Amos as a pattern, came to America—or to any western nation—and picked one inhuman, violent, bloody sin that is officially permitted and widely practiced among us, what sin would that be? What one sin would God use to define our nation's deeper, corrupted character and our compromised conscience? What if God were to say to us, "America, in you is sin, sin, sin, and your character has become so degenerate and corrupt that now you even (and here God names one sin)—therefore, you are judged and condemned."

What One Sin Would God Name?

Our nation must face this question, for the time of our retribution is fast approaching. God calls people into judgment collectively in their national capacity, and this is something America's founding fathers firmly believed. "We cannot claim to be God's pets, " Billy Graham warned. "We have no dispensation from judgment. If we continue in our present course, the moral law that says 'the wages of sin is death'[12] will mean the ultimate death of our society."[13]

The belief that God does not regard our actions is an atheistic concept, like Judah's attitude when they ridiculed the prophets who warned them. Judah said, "He will do nothing! No harm will come to us; we will never see sword or famine. The prophets are but wind."[14]

But if we are guilty—and we are—of the sins of the six pagan nations, and the sins of Israel and Judah, we must *know* that God is warning us, "Prepare to meet your God."[15] And He is the God that America professes to trust. We are accountable to Him. Our nation has seen many disasters, but the things that God has already chastised us with are nothing in comparison to what we may expect from His hands if we continue in our sins, continue to provoke Him. The sins that brought the chastisements upon us have been great, but our obstinate impenitence under those chastisements— which were intended to reform us and bring us back to God—is a certain sign of our ultimate downfall. Our nation will not be delivered unless there is national repentance. We cannot continue to treat with contempt the rich mercies and grace that God has bestowed on us.

Abraham Lincoln spoke to the U.S. Congress about the Civil War, and its implications for the nation, and said, "The struggle of today is not altogether for today; it is for the vast future ahead."

And so it is now—answering the question of our sins is not altogether for today, it is for the vast future still ahead, the future in which our children and their children and their children's children will live. But unless we *do* answer the question of our sins, and answer it rightly, then like the nations in Amos's time, neither we nor our children will have a vast future.

The countdown has started. When will it end, when will our time run out? In Bern, Switzerland, there is a message over the entrance of Loeb's department store, *"Nur noch 3,427 tage bis zum Jahre* 2000." The interpretation is, "Only 3,427 days until the year 2000." Will we make it to the year 2000? Are we numbering our days? Israel didn't. Judah didn't. The pagan nations didn't.

Are we?

GOD IS!

---

[1] John Fleming, *Religious Decline and Its Consequences,* (La Trobe University, Bundoora, Vic, Australia), p. 15.

[2] Ibid., p. 32.

[3] Amos 1:2.

[4] Hebrews 12:5-11.

[5] Amos 3:2 (NKJV).

[6] Amos 3:10.

[7] Amos 9:10b.

[8] Amos 9:8.

[9] Francis Foulkes, *God's Message to the Nation,* (West Africa: Africa Christian Press, 1977), p. 6.

[10] Ron Buckland, *Amos: A Mini-Commentary,* (HomeBush West, NSW, Australia: Anzea Books, 1972), p. 6.

[11] Romans 2:11.

[12] Romans 6:23.

[13] Billy Graham, *World Aflame,* (Fleming H. Revell, 1965), p. 91.

[14] Jeremiah 5:12-13a.

[15] Amos 4:12.

3

Defining Sins

Empire Rome shall perish—write that word
In the blood that she hath spilt;
Perish hopeless and abhorred,
Deep in ruin as in guilt.[1]

S. Conway

Their feet are swift to shed blood; . . .
There is no fear of God before their eyes.[2]

A boy about five years old was riding with his mother in their car. They were following a truck filled with trash. For some reason, the men in the truck had not tied down the large canvas used to cover the trash, so one of the men was laying on top of it to hold it down. The boy stared intently through the car's windshield at the man's still, lifeless-looking body. As the truck moved along ahead of their car, a gust of wind blew up a corner of the canvas and the man on top quickly moved over and pushed it down into place. When the man moved, the boy was horrified and exclaimed to his mother, "Mummy, look! They've thrown away a perfectly good man!"

Such a childish observation and comment might make us smile a bit. But we can't smile at all when we think of the fact that every day we throw away perfectly good human beings in our nation's abortion clinics—and in abortion clinics in every western nation.

Killing the unborn is the sin God has surely picked to define us, and because of that sin He is saying to us, *"America (or any nation), your character is so corrupt and your conscience so callous that you can, without qualm, reach into the womb and kill helpless and innocent unborn children—for this sin I have judged you, and you are condemned!"* Our great peril is that we have so seared our conscience that we cannot understand the enormity of what we have done and are doing. We continue to kill—and as each slain child cries out to Him, God moves His wrathful hand closer to us.

It is a sign of our times that some abortionists actually believe that abortion is murder, and yet continue to perform them for reasons they justify to themselves. Dr. Robert Jones of Australia is one of these amazing abortionists. He explains his justification for doing them in this way, "One has to start with the attitude that you accept the criticism that this is murder. Abortion is murder—I agree with that. You're extinguishing life, and if you don't face up to that, you're not being honest with yourself. If you face the fact you're doing murder, and you know you're doing it for good reason, then you can be relaxed about it. It is justifiable murder, if there is such a thing. It is the lesser of two evils."[3] Those statements will take several readings to find the illogical logic in them, especially "justifiable murder."

God, however, is not justifying the murder of unborn children—not for any of man's reasons. We now openly possess—and openly justify—one of the things the Lord hates, "hands that shed innocent blood."[4] Where once the womb was the source and haven of new life, it is now the least-safe place for unborn children—none of them know if they will be allowed to make it through the nine months that God has decreed they must spend there. In our God-professing nation, abortion has become the leading cause of death. The womb has become a tomb!

Throughout the world, approximately fifty million unborn children are destroyed every year.[5]

That much bloodshed is staggering, horrifying, for it means that this twentieth century is the bloodiest century in the history of our world. And because of the television media, we are a society that has seen more bloodshed than any other—so much, in fact, that we are fast becoming insensitive to it. The fallout from this desensitization has been devastating. Diane Culbertson of *USA Today* wrote, "Abortion has wreaked havoc on this nation. The family as an institution has been weakened. Too many men have regarded abortion as the solution to a 'mistake' and have walked away from their responsibilities as fathers. Too many women have casually looked at abortion as just another form of birth control instead of the taking of a life."[6]

We are a generation that is rapidly losing even the smallest measure of respect for human life. In one of his books, John Updike wrote that death, once invited in, leaves its footprints everywhere. How appallingly true this is of abortion!

With abortion, our own holocaust is raging, and the womb is the chamber of destruction. We are practicing genocide on a new race of human beings called "the unborn." Our heavenly Father sees each one of those fifty million unborn babies that are cruelly and mercilessly destroyed each year. Fifty million abortions a year are fifty million individual human beings made in God's own image—each an unrepeatable miracle—snuffed out of existence as if they were only animals. And fifty million times a year God is pained, one time after another, as He sees each one of His miracles of life rejected and destroyed—His pain never subsides, and He never "gets used to it," as we have. We turn our heads and hearts from the carnage, but God never does; the human destruction is always before Him.

Our ready acceptance of abortion demonstrates our willing belief in clever lies. As the Apostle Paul stated, we "invent ways of doing evil."[7] Our abortion technology gives us the means to make the killing of unborn babies assembly-line quick—thus our modern society has become more efficient in destroying God's newest life than the Nazis were in destroying God's oldest people, the Jews. The spirit of Molech[8] lives, and America's land is polluted by the shedding of innocent blood.

In our nation, killing is quickly becoming an acceptable solution to difficult problems. You have an unwanted pregnancy? Simple, kill the "fetus," and be careful you don't make a mistake and call it a "baby," or you might not be able to kill it without bothering your conscience. Are you old and in pain or having physical problems you don't want to handle? Simple again, kill yourself or have someone else do it for you—only don't call it "suicide," call it "euthanasia" so it sounds better. Who's next? The feeble, the handicapped, the mentally disturbed, the socially unacceptable? Once the killing has started, its easier to continue than it is to stop. Our culture has become a culture of killing, and violence has become an everyday occurrence that is hardly worth noticing.

We must face what the Word of God has to say about the shedding of innocent blood. "Hear the word of Lord, you Israelites, because the Lord has a charge to bring against you who live in the land: 'There is no faithfulness, no love, no acknowledgment of God in the land. There is only cursing, lying and murder, stealing and adultery; they break all bounds, and BLOODSHED

FOLLOWS BLOODSHED.'"[9] (Emphasis mine).

Here God speaks through the prophet Hosea and says that Israel's sins are breaking all bounds like a flooding river, without restraint and out of control; nothing but sin, sin, sin; wave after wave of sin. Then He points to one sin in particular: BLOODSHED, and uses this sin to show the magnitude of Israel's iniquity. "Bloodshed follows bloodshed" is the language of wanton excess. Here is how one commentator described it:

> The term *Damim* (the Hebrew word for "blood-shed") we propose, probably refers to the shedding of innocent blood by official sanction, and the crime charged against the nation here, as elsewhere, is the formal sacrifice of human beings, in particular children who are innocent and unblemished . . . . In any event, the shedding of innocent blood is an ultimate crime . . . it symbolizes the ultimate rebellion against God in the destruction of human beings who are made in His image . . . this phrase relates specifically to the ritual sacrifice of human beings, especially children, and hence involves both leadership and people in a common and universal guilt.[10]

R. C. Sproul, commenting on the following passage from Exodus, says, "Scripture indicates that God commanded the death penalty for fetus-killing in Israel:

> If men fight, and hurt a woman with child, so that she gives birth prematurely, yet no harm follows, he shall surely be punished accordingly as the woman's husband imposes on him; and he shall pay as the judges *determine*. But if *any* harm follows, then you shall give life for life.[11]

Sproul then explained the meaning of this passage, "God taught Israel that abortion was murder. Therefore, He assigned the appropriate punishment. As in all forms of murder, that punishment was death."[12]

Pinpointing the seriousness of abortion, Gleason L. Archer, in his *Encyclopedia of Bible Difficulties,* says,

> Psalm 139 indicates very definitely that God's personal regard for the embryo begins from the time of its inception . . . . Even though many thousands of embryos and fetuses are deliberately aborted every year throughout the world, God cares about the unborn and takes personal knowledge of them just as truly before they are born as after their delivery . . . . Therefore anyone who does takes the life of any human being at any stage in that life's career will have to reckon with God . . . . When does an embryo begin to be a creature made in the image of God? From the moment of conception in the womb, Scripture says. Therefore God will require his (the baby's) blood at the hands of his murderer, whether the abortionist be a medical doctor or a non-professional.[13]

The value expressed was once preeminent in our society. Human life was sacred. But in recent years, contrary views have infected us, and we now are wavering between that value and a conflicting one. A recent editorial cartoon illustrates our situation. It shows a car's rear bumper. On one end of the bumper, a bumper sticker reads, "Save the Whales!" On the other end, another bumper sticker reads, "Abort the Babies!"

Another editorial cartoon shows two pictures. One picture has people applauding those who were protesting the killing of dolphins, the other shows people applauding the police as they drag to jail those who were protesting in front of an abortion clinic.

Still another editorial cartoon shows a woman sitting in an abortion-clinic waiting room, awaiting the procedure (or whatever it's called). The unborn child in her womb is shown thinking, "I wish I were a whale!"

Conflicting values—save animals and the environment, kill unborn babies. For the one, protection—for the other, bloodshed.

We are split over abortion. Being split over this horrible sin, however, is not our greatest problem or danger—fence-sitting is.

What has happened to us is that a vicious, Satanic, lie has slowly slithered its way into our national consciousness until we have come to believe it. It's a lie that says it is virtuous to be morally neutral—the lie is called PRO-CHOICE. Pro-choice is societal fence-sitting. Sproul has called pro-choice "the moral cop-out of our day—the shame of our churches and their leaders. It is time to get off the fence."[14]

The pro-choice argument is used to rationalize killing in the womb and other sins—it is a defining lie that is used to justify a defining sin. It is a public heresy that numbs our public conscience by making us feel honorable as we stand on the sidelines.

A pro-choice position does not absolve us of accountability for the bloodshed that is rampant in our midst. The shedding of innocent blood is specifically connected with God's pronouncements of national judgment. Manasseh, the wicked king of Judah, "also shed so much innocent blood that he filled Jerusalem from end to end—besides the sin that he had caused Judah to commit, so that they did evil in the eyes of the Lord."[15]

Years later, when Judah fell under the judgment of God, the Scriptures say, "Surely these things happened to Judah according to the Lord's command, in order to remove them from his presence because of the sins of Manasseh and all he had done, including the shedding of innocent blood. For he had filled Jerusalem with innocent blood, and the Lord was not willing to forgive."[16]

Psalm 106 confirms the reason for God's judgment:

> They sacrificed their sons and their daughters to
> demons. They shed innocent blood, the blood of their
> sons and daughters, whom they sacrificed to the idols
> of Canaan, and the land was desecrated by their
> blood . . . . Therefore the LORD was angry with his
> people and abhorred his inheritance. He handed
> them over to the nations, and their foes ruled over
> them.[17]

Speaking through the prophet Jeremiah, God said,
"For they have forsaken me and made this a place of
foreign gods; . . . and they have filled this place with
the blood of the innocent."[18] In His judgment on Edom,
God was specific as to their punishment, "I will give
you over to bloodshed and it will pursue you."[19]

In the Book of Joel there is the same theme: "But
Egypt will be desolate, Edom a desert waste, because
of violence done to the people of Judah, in whose land
they shed innocent blood."[20] And eight times, Ezekiel
22 refers to the shedding of blood when Jerusalem faces
judgment. In the Book of Jeremiah, God says, "Do no
wrong or violence to the alien, the fatherless or the
widow, and do not shed innocent blood in this place."[21]

Bloodshed. Forbidden by God. The Scriptures
shout this out over and over again until we cannot miss
it or deny it or ignore it.

The Arabs say that the dew of heaven will not
descend on a spot that has been watered with innocent
blood. Said Isaiah, "See, the Lord is coming out of his
dwelling to punish the people of the earth for their sins.
The earth will disclose the blood shed upon her; she
will conceal her slain no longer."[22]

It ought to frighten us to realize that every killing
of human life, however secret, will be brought into
God's light—every killer, however unsuspected and

unfound, will be exposed before God and punished—
and every innocent victim will be avenged by the
almighty Creator of heaven and earth. Our heavenly
Father hears the cry of each unborn baby that we have
destroyed; they cry, one after another, like Abel's blood,
for vengeance. We pay no attention to their cries, we
simply drown them in the swamp of our worthless
rhetoric and debate, but the cries of the slain unborn
reach to heaven, and they are getting louder and more
plaintive in their Father's ears. If we on earth continue
to ignore their cries, those cries will come crashing down
on us in a torrent of judgment.

Evangelist Charles G. Finney, who was part of the
Great American Awakening in the nineteenth century,
was outspoken in his opposition to slavery. He voiced
the cry of the slaves in a moving challenge to the Church:

> Every southern breeze is loaded down with the
> cries of lamentation, mourning, and woe. Two
> millions of degraded [slaves] in our own land stretch
> their hands, all shackled and bleeding, and send forth
> to the Church of God the agonizing cry for help. And
> shall the Church, in her efforts to reclaim and save
> the world, deafen her ears to this voice of agony and
> despair? God forbid! The Church cannot turn away
> from this question . . . . God will push it to a decision
> . . . . It is in vain to account it an act of piety to turn
> away the ear from hearing this cry of distress.[23]

When something, such as the message of this book,
is branded as being alarmist, many shut their ears and
hearts to it. But as a nation we have reason to be
alarmed. The killing of our unborn children is not a
political or social issue—it is a grave moral question that
defines us as a nation and has enormous implications for
us. We dare not minimize those implications. I say
again, WE DARE NOT MINIMIZE THOSE IMPLI-
CATIONS! For God will not and does not.

Who is accountable before God for this bloodshed in our midst? The whole nation—not just the woman who has the abortion or the doctor who performs it. Within out nation, however, there are several groups that will have to give a special accounting to God:

> •The fathers of the babies who are aborted. The heavenly Father is calling earthly fathers to give account for the ongoing destruction of their unborn children.

> •The lawmakers, judges, and politicians who make laws and rule on them in such a way as to promote and permit abortion.

> •The physicians, nurses, clinic staff members, and all those who assist in the killings in any way. Compounding their guilt will be the fact that they take money for it, lots of money, and the most damning kind of blood-money!

> •Those who promote the alleged right of a woman to an abortion, such as feminists, many members of the media, and some environmentalists.

> •The pastors, ministers, priests, and church leaders who have remained silent while the holocaust of the unborn rages on. This silence is complicity in the killings. By their silence they give their tacit agreement to the crime. What each church needs is a white-hot pulpit with a preacher who is aflame with the heart of God, and who boldly proclaims the Word of the Lord and speaks deeply to this society. When there is fire in the pulpit, there will be fire in the pews!

Abortion is not the only sin that defines our society, however. Homosexual perversion ranks alongside abortion in defining us. It is a sad commentary on our generation that America and most nations in the West are moving toward the acceptance of homosexual practices, including sodomy—the perverted sin for which God destroyed Sodom. Many of our highest elected officials are working to raise homosexuality to the status of a third sex, and even allowing it and encouraging it to be so presented in our tax-funded public schools. Many of our wonderful politicians are also pushing for gays to be accepted in the military, and they belittle those whose morality opposes sodomy—and the other degrading homosexual practices—by calling them homophobic. Name-calling has replaced Christian decency.

Moreover, and even more telling, legal means are being sought to bring this about. Laws in many places, for example, now force a landlord to rent to a homosexual couple when they apply for a rental. The right of decent citizens to make moral distinctions is more and more being denied.

Many consider societal approval of abortion and homosexual sin to be progress. They consider these to be basic civil rights under the constitution that was written by our nation's godly forefathers. But God doesn't call these sins "civil rights." He calls them murder and perversion. Abortion has been termed by some to be the greatest moral issue of modern times, and now homosexual perversion must be considered as a part of the same darkness.

During the national debate on the plan to lift the ban on homosexuals in the American military, the Assemblies of God Commission on Chaplains issued a statement that strongly opposed it. The statement concluded with a penetrating and accurate comment: "We plead with our leaders to abandon their efforts to lift the ban on homosexuality in the military LEST SUCH A FLAGRANT VIOLATION OF GOD'S LAWS SHOULD SUBJECT OUR BELOVED HOMELAND AND ITS CITIZENS TO GOD'S RETRIBUTION AND WRATH" (Emphasis mine).

It is essential that we understand, and deeply implant into our national conscience, the truth that putting our government's stamp of approval on homosexual activity is not a trivial matter, not something to be glossed over or hidden under the cover of "civil rights." Homosexual activity is the sin of "shameful lust" that the Holy Spirit condemned through the writings of the inspired Apostle Paul.[24] It is that to which God gave over a defiant society. True, homosexuality is not the only sexual sin, but it's a watershed perversion that showcases our greater depravity.

In fact, within the categories of violence and immorality, abortion and homosexual sins are "touchstone sins." They stand as the most base levels of degradation in the categories they represent. We might find this hard to believe because these sins are so commonly accepted today, but the fact that they are so widely accepted gives credence to this evaluation. It isn't only that they are practiced—that is bad enough—but they are approved by society. This makes them preeminently dangerous to us, because by enjoying such respectable positions, these sins have easy access to us and particularly to our children. They have, therefore, virtually free rein to work their evil and bring condemnation upon us—and this is what is happening in our society today.

To those who have had abortions or to those who are struggling against homosexual desires, we need to proclaim, and do proclaim, that there is forgiveness, deliverance, and healing in Jesus Christ if they will repent of their sins, confess them to Him, ask His forgiveness, and make Him the Lord of their lives.

Our public acceptance of these sins is a major spiritual issue. Abortion and homosexual perversion define our collective deeper rebellion against God and they reveal our degree of self-centeredness and self-absorption. With both sins we are playing with loaded guns. The conservative and liberal politicians in our country are making the same mistake; they are trying to fix our social system without realizing that the system is cursed. It is cursed with the blood of over thirty million unborn children who have been killed in this nation alone, and it is cursed in that it is pushing for acceptance of homosexual perversion. Such a system cannot be blessed by God—and unless God blesses it, it will never be fixed.

We are fools if we believe any lying words that tell us our social system can be fixed, or that it will be blessed by God without national repentance.

The Scriptures and history tell us otherwise.

They tell us the truth.

Let us start listening to them, and stop listening to lies.

---

[1] S. Conway, *The Revelation of St. John the Divine, Pulpit Commentary*, (Eerdmans, Grand Rapids, MI, 1950), p. 253.

[2] Romans 3:15, 18.

[3] Dr. Robert Jones, Adelaide, Australia, quoted in *Good Weekend Magazine*, (*The Age* newspaper, Melbourne, April 6, 1991), p. 21.

[4] Proverbs 6:17b.

[5] From a report by the American Worldwatch Institute, quoted in the *Tages-Anzeiger* newspaper, Switzerland, Monday, July 6, 1990.

[6] Diane Culbertson, *USA Today*, October 6, 1991.

[7] Romans 1:30.

[8] Leviticus 18:21. A detestable Semitic deity honored by the sacrifice of children.

[9] Hosea 4:1-2.

[10] Anderson and Freedman, pp. 338-339.

[11]Exodus 21:22-23 (NKJV).

[12]R. C. Sproul, *Tabletalk*, Orlando, FL, May, 1991, p. 24.

[13]Gleason L. Archer, *Encyclopedia of Bible Difficulties*, (Zondervan, Grand Rapids, MI, 1982), pp. 246-247.

[14]R. C. Sproul, *Ethics and the Christian*, (Tyndale House, 1983), p. 87.

[15]2 Kings 21:16.

[16]2 Kings 24:3-4.

[17]Psalm 106:37-41.

[18]Jeremiah 19:4.

[19]Ezekiel 35:6.

[20]Joel 3:19.

[21]Jeremiah 22:3.

[22]Isaiah 26:21.

[23]Charles G. Finney, *Revivals of Religion*, (Fleming H., Revell Co.), p. 322.

[24]Romans 1:26.

4

Our Fatherless Generation

A father to the fatherless, a defender of widows,
is God in his holy dwelling.[1]

He defends the cause of the fatherless and the
widow.[2]

If homosexual perversion and killing our unborn
are defining sins of our generation, if AIDS is a defining
disease, then an errant manhood is our defining
delinquency. We are heading toward the abyss of
judgment, and an errant manhood is the edge of the
cliff. Our defining crisis is a fatherless generation.

I've asked myself this question, "If I were a
cartoonist, and I wanted to draw just one cartoon that
would most accurately depict our modern moment,
what would I draw?" What slice of our contemporary
world would I use to illustrate where we are today in
our values, in our sin, and where we are headed? What
would I portray? Without question there are many that
I could portray, but here is my submission—I would
draw a cartoon with two parts. On the left I would
show a young, unmarried woman, pushing a baby

carriage down a city street. On the right I would show a young, unmarried woman sitting in an abortion clinic, waiting for the abortionist to kill her unborn baby. Under the cartoon would be the caption, "WHERE ARE THE FATHERS?"

Every man, young or old, Christian or not, when he sees a single woman raising a baby, or walking into an abortion clinic, should cringe in shame, because what he is witnessing is a tragic testimony to the collective delinquency of men.

The late Francis Schaeffer said that the cry of our world is, "Is there anybody at home in the universe?" This is really a call for a father—our heavenly Father.

The cry for a father is today's silent yearning. It was mine as I grew up. I haven't seen my real father since I was about six, when he left his family. My only memories of him are ones of drunkenness, violence, and immorality. After my father left my mother, they were divorced, and she married again, a hard-working but atheistic man. I feel very fortunate that in spite of this I became a Christian when I was eleven. I have a good mother, and God gave me a fine, beautiful wife. The Lord kept me from the sins of my fathers—it was as if He lifted me out of the fire before I was ever in it. I did, however, have some great fathering; it came from a very godly great-grandfather who as a boy had immigrated from Switzerland to America with his parents—this book is dedicated to his memory.

The silent yearning by so many for a father is really a cry for someone to want us, nurture us, protect us, as only a good father can, particularly a biological one. And certainly now, with mother also gone out of the home, the cry has added significance.

Our defining sin today is that we have created a fatherless generation—a fatherless generation both in the womb and out of the womb. As much as any single condition can, this determines where we are as a society.

As said in a previous chapter, one of the fastest growing groups today is single-parent families, with most of these headed by women—women without husbands and children without fathers. And tragically, well-meant but misguided welfare dollars are often used to support such fatherlessness. The devastating effect on our future from an enlarging segment of our society growing up without a father, particularly in our ghettos, is immeasurable. Adding to this deplorable situation is that increasingly there are homes where the mother and father are not married, just living together, and homes where the children are not the biological offspring of one of the partners, usually the man. As a result, there is an increasing number of homes in which men are raising other men's children while other men raise theirs. In addition, in those homes where the biological children are living with their actual parents, the fathers many times are struggling with their fatherhood. We want to help fathers, give them ideas and encouragement, so there is a chapter in this book especially for them: "Give Us Fathers."

Our fatherless generation is part of an unwanted generation. The 40s produced the *postwar generation,* the 50s the *silent generation,* the 60s the *dropout generation,* the 70s the *rebellious generation,* the 80s the *self-centered yuppie generation*—and now, in the 90s, we are reaping the fruit of those generations, and we are producing the *unwanted generation.* From abortion to child abuse, from careers to life-style, the message we give our children is, "We don't want you!" That is, unless it's convenient for us. We'll allow you to be born at our convenience, but if you're conceived when it's not convenient, we'll destroy you—and if we've allowed you to be born, we'll spend time with you when it's convenient for us. Our children are learning this message, and we're naive if we think they're not.

Our peril is enormous because of this situation. But

it is the fatherless generation that we've created IN THE WOMB that is particularly damning to us. In America, and most western countries we've removed every unborn child from the protection of his or her father. We've blindly and stubbornly embraced the pro-choice "right" of a woman to have an abortion if she chooses— we insist it is her decision and her decision alone to kill or not kill the life in her womb. And we've decreed that the father of the unborn child, whether married to the mother or not, has no legal part in any abortion decision. This has become a part of our public dogma. In June, 1992, the United States Supreme Court—a court that should have been conservative—made this stance official. Ruling on a Pennyslvania law, they struck down the requirement that a wife has to notify her husband before she has an abortion. Today in the land of the free and the brave, a father cannot keep his unborn child from being killed.

Every unborn child, therefore, is legally fatherless.

FATHERLESS! Our peril because of this is frightening. This fact alone, when we comprehend its seriousness, should put men on their faces in repentance before God, their heavenly Father, beseeching Him for mercy on this country, on their unborn children, and on them.

Abortion defines us and adding to that sin the grave offense of making our unborn fatherless and unprotected as well, immeasurably increases our blame and our judgment. The heavenly Father deeply cares for the fatherless. The Psalmist wrote of the Lord, "You . . . listen to their cry, defending the fatherless . . . ."[3] Over and again, God told His people to care for the aliens, the widows, and the fatherless—the three weakest groups in society. The idolatrous, pagan nations were brutal and insensitive to human life. God tells His people to be different, to take care of the very weakest and give them protection. Our heavenly Father demands justice for the fatherless, and if earthly fathers will not speak up for them, He will. *And His voice will be heard!*

One of God's key evaluations of a nation is, HOW WELL DOES IT TAKE CARE OF THE VERY WEAKEST? This is one of the reasons God instituted government. He gave the state "the sword" to protect human life and guard and defend the weakest. When a nation abdicates that fundamental and vital role, it also abdicates its right to exist, and its judgment is thereby assured.

Here is what scholar-theologian-author R. C. Sproul says in his comment on Exodus 22:22-24:

> God told the Israelites they must not oppress widows and orphans (or more literally, the fatherless). Throughout the Bible God manifests a ferocious concern for women and children who do not have husbands and fathers. . . . God will be a Husband for the widow and a Father for the fatherless, and His jealousy will burn with fury if those under His special protection are mistreated. God told Israel that just as He heard their cry when they were oppressed in Egypt, so He would hear the cry of the widow and fatherless. Just as He destroyed the Egyptian oppressor, so He would destroy them if they oppressed widows and orphans.[4]

It is not an overstatement to say that America is in danger—in fact, it is more likely an understatement. Even worse, our danger is double—God cares for the fatherless AND THE WIDOWS. When we in our obstinate emphasis contend that it is the exclusive right of a woman to decide whether she has an abortion, we set the pregnant woman alone and isolate her from the father of her child. We make her effectively a widow—and many women, pregnant, struggling and vulnerable, have felt that isolation. Now, of course, rebellious feminists want it that way; and if they get what they want, they will have much to answer for—and God will give them what they do not want.

In addition, the exclusive "right" of a woman to an abortion has become so much a part of our public doctrine that we have extended the right to any female of any age. Many states today let an underage girl decide for herself whether to have an abortion without her parents' knowledge and consent. This makes the girl fatherless. The baby in her womb is fatherless— and so is she! Our society constantly compounds its indictments.

Feminist philosophy has greatly contributed to fatherlessness. When women, in the name of liberation, joined so willingly in the so-called sexual revolution, they helped tear down a vital social precept that helped build our society. That precept was that A WOMAN SHOULD HAVE SEX ONLY WITH THE MAN TO WHOM SHE IS MARRIED. Men have an equal role in insisting on this precept, and they are not excused as we shall see. In the relationship between the sexes, however, women have a *vital* role, and when they readily had sex outside of marriage, they helped open the floodgates to much of the moral and social chaos we have today.

That age-old serpent cleverly brought his temptation to feminist Eves, promising freedom from the strictures of having sex only in the bonded covenant of marriage. "Men are the oppressors," he whispered, "there is a double-standard; men are allowed to sexually roam while women are expected to stay chastely at home, bear children, be homemakers." Our modern Eves ate the forbidden fruit—followed eagerly by our modern Adams, who loved the idea of sex-without-responsibility—having the fruit without having to take care of the orchard. Now we suffer the consequences in an exploding out-of-wedlock birthrate, abortion, moral uncertainty, family breakdown—and children in homes without fathers. Considering everything, it doesn't take much logic to draw a connection between increased fatherlessness and increased violence. With men turning their backs on the fatherless, society is left completely uncovered and unguarded, and we can only expect the raging violence against the young, and by the young, to rapidly rise.

As it turned out, however, and much to the chagrin of the women, they did not gain the sexual equality they naively thought they would—they only encouraged the playboy mentality in men. As B. A. Santamaria observed, "Women's liberation in theory has been men's liberation in practice."[5] A woman can expound to a man on her right to be sexually liberated, it's her body and all, and the man will readily agree—and chuckle all the way to her bed. Many disillusioned women have seen the sudden end of a relationship they trusted, and the disappearance of their boyfriend, once they were pregnant. The real tragedy in this is that so many younger women are growing up without a moral anchor.

In spite of what women have done, it is the men who bear primary responsibility before God for the situation of our country and families. It is the men who will be first before God's bar of accountability. It is true that Eve sinned before Adam, but when God dealt with them, He started and finished with Adam. Today, God will start first with our prodigal Adams, not our sinning Eves. Some have said that feminism has emasculated men. Wrong! Men have castrated themselves.

Men need to take a hard look at the evils of our world—child molestation, violence in our streets, violence in our schools, robberies, muggings, carjackings, stabbings, murders, rapes, wife-beatings, pornography, homosexual perversion, ad nauseam. Look at them all. These evils are predominately committed by men—both young and old. They are evils of our gender. We are the ones who are doing them. Look particularly at the fatherless homes. THEY ARE FATHERLESS BECAUSE WE ARE NOT THERE! Look at our unborn children being destroyed every day by the millions while we sit idly by, excusing ourselves with everything from work to sports. We have left unprotected our unborn children that we conceived.

Men must come to grips with this and see the seriousness of what they are doing—and not doing— FROM GOD'S POINT OF VIEW. They have become "the wicked" in Psalm 94 who delude themselves and "pour out arrogant words." Now they "slay the widow and . . . murder the fatherless."[6] Yet they cavalierly say, "The Lord does not see; the God of Jacob pays no heed." But hear the Lord's chilling response, "Does he who formed the eye not see? Does he who disciplines nations not punish?"[7]

Read also what is written in Psalm 9:12: "For he who avenges blood remembers; he does not ignore the cry of the afflicted." Then in Psalm 10 it is written, "But you, O God, . . . you are the helper of the fatherless . . . . You hear, O Lord, the desire of the afflicted; you . . . listen to their cry, defending the fatherless and the oppressed, in order that man, who is of the earth, may terrify no more."[8] And through Isaiah the prophet, God indicted Judah, "Your hands are full of blood, . . ." and commanded them, "Defend the cause of the fatherless."[9]

The Book of Job records that Job knew how much God cared for the fatherless, for he said to Him, "If I have raised my hand against the fatherless, knowing that I had influence in court, then let my arm fall from the shoulder."[10] We can imagine that if Job were alive now, he would use his influence in our courts on behalf of the fatherless—he would speak up for them rather than against them as so many men are doing today.

Men would do well to take heed of Job's reason for not raising his hand against the fatherless: "For I dreaded destruction from God, and for fear of his splendor I could not do such things."[11]

Modern men have lost their fear of God and their fear of having to account to Him for their lives and the lives of the fatherless. Regardless of their modern arrogance, however, they can be certain of one thing—when they stand before the Great White Throne of God to be judged, they will quickly regain their fear.

Every earthly father will face the heavenly Father to give answer for the blood of each of the millions of babies that have been aborted. "Father" means the giver and protector of life—and regardless of the importance of the mother's role, the buck stops with the father. Every man will give a personal accounting for every act of sexual intercourse he has ever had and the consequences of that intercourse. And he will give account to almighty God for every aborted baby that he fathered. The root cause of the problem is sexual, and any man who has ignored the responsibility of his sexuality should turn to the heavenly Father in humility and repentance and ask Him for wisdom and courage to be a godly man and father. Go to the Father to be a father.

The opening words of the Lord's Prayer are, "Our Father, which art in heaven . . . ." The heavenly Father, who cares even for sparrows and lilies and grass, cares deeply for all human life and especially for life that is helpless and innocent. The unborn is the most helpless of the helpless, the most innocent of the innocent. Though they are still in the sanctuary of the womb, their heavenly Father looks upon each one of them as innocent, as sacred, as life from Him. He demands that all earthly fathers do the same!

Daily around the world, women abort their unborn, the children of men. Society tells them it is right, normal and moral for them to kill the innocent human life developing helplessly in their wombs. The cry of the unborn today most certainly is, "Where is my father?" It's a cry that should scream in our ears—as it does in God's. To God, their blood cries for vengeance and their heavenly Father hears. Their collective cries are fast becoming a thundering crescendo that He will surely soon answer in judgment of those who are making His children cry.

Most men are skeptical of simplistic-sounding theories, but today's crisis is the crisis of manhood. At the root of today's plight, for whatever reasons, is men's moral and spiritual failure. The only answer to today's crucial challenges is to raise up "men mighty in spirit" who know God. When we remedy the manhood problem, we cut the roots of other problems like abortion, pornography, drug addiction, homosexual perversion, and family breakdown.

Our delinquency in abandoning our unborn is the final checkpoint ushering in our judgment when a just God, responding to the cry of the aborted unborn fatherless, rises to take action! For creating a fatherless generation, we are in great peril of a judgment that we deserve. If our society goes over the cliff, it will be errant men who have pushed it.

Fatherlessness defines America.

I pray the gravity of this will sink in and impel every father who reads this to go on his face before God in repentance. We must entreat our Lord for mercy and for a spiritual awakening. We must determine to be the men and fathers we were created and called to be.

Fathers, let's lead our nation back to God.

While there is still time.

---

[1]Psalm 68:5.
[2]Deuteronomy 10:18.

[3]Psalm 10:17-18.
[4]R. C. Sproul, *Tabletalk*, Orlando, FL, May, 1991, p. 27.
[5]R. A. Santamaria, *The Australian*, January 16, 1990.
[6]Psalm 94:4, 6.
[7]Psalm 94:7, 9-10.
[8]Psalm 10:14, 17-18.
[9]Isaiah 1:15, 17.
[10]Job 31:21-22.
[11]Job 31:23.

5

The Apathetic Enemy

Science may have found a cure for most evils; but it has found no remedy for the worst of them all—the apathy of human beings.

Helen Keller[1]

The crack in the moral dam is widening, but like the people in Noah's day before the flood, life goes on as usual with only a few concerned and scarcely anyone alarmed. However, apathy will not deter catastrophe. The people of Noah's day were not expecting judgment—but it came!

Billy Graham[2]

The minister slammed his hand down on the pulpit and shouted, "The trouble with the Church today is lack of knowledge and apathy!" Then he expounded on the subject for forty-five minutes. When he finished, he looked down at one of his deacons in the first row and said, "What do you think of that, George?"

George looked lazily up him and said, "I don't know, pastor, and I don't care."

That story reflects an experience I had on my first trip to Australia. I'd been there only a short time on a journey that would take me across the nation. My host for the first few days was a delightful gentleman of seventy-four. One day he grinned at me and asked if I knew what the major problem was in Australia. I shook my head. His grin widened as he announced, "The big problem in Australia is described in a bit of graffiti I saw. It read, 'The problem in Australia is apathy!' But someone had scrawled underneath, 'So what?'" I laughed and told him that was the problem in America, also. People don't know—and if they do, they don't care. As the cartoon character Pogo said, "We have met the enemy, and the enemy is us!"

Some feel that in western nations, just before everything ends, there will be a big yawn. One commentator wryly observed, "Prophets don't talk in their sleep, they talk in other people's sleep!"

The prophet Amos had to talk while Israel slept. But they were busy sleepers—spiritual sleepers usually are. With the peace and prosperity they were experiencing went activity—going here, doing that, building something. Jesus would have spoken of it as an "eating and drinking, marrying and giving in marriage" kind of atmosphere. It was an intoxicating time. There were plenty of leisure activities. In fact, Amos probably appeared on the scene during one of their festivals, which is undoubtedly why they didn't like his bringing God's Word to them—it put a damper on fleshly fun.

In 1784, President George Washington, when proclaiming the first national thanksgiving feast, said he feared "the arrogance of prosperity" for the young United States. He expressed concern that God "imprint on our hearts a deep and solemn sense of our obligations to Him for [these blessings]; to teach us rightly to estimate their immense value; to preserve us from the arrogance of prosperity and from hazarding the advantages we enjoy by delusive pursuits . . . ."[3] Wise words.

In Amos's time, Israel did not know she was hazarding the wonderful advantages she enjoyed by engaging in those things that kept her mind off God. Spiritual sleepers rarely do. So to get the attention of the prosperous distracted nation, God thundered through Amos, "The LORD ROARS out of Zion . . . ." The roar of a lion is a most terrifying sound in the dark, so the Lord's words came as a lion's roar to rivet the attention of His people, to make them hear His words above all the dark sounds in their nation. Once God had their attention, Amos wasted no time—the situation was too serious—but got straight to the point with all the power of an anointed prophet. GOD IS SPEAKING! YOU FACE JUDGMENT! With a bluntness common to the Old Testament prophets of God, Amos came straight at them with the Word of God.

Bible scholars describe Amos as one of the fiercest, if not *the* fiercest, prophet in the Scriptures. But fierce as compared to what? Fierce, if compared to the easeful sounds Israel's ears were used to, but raising the voice to the level of a lion's roar was exactly what God needed to wake Israel to the consequences they faced if they did not turn from their sins. Getting the attention of apathetic people is difficult, and the Lord used strong words to do it. Often when His people turned from Him to other gods and other ways, God called them "harlots." God calling them that always had the same jolting effect that a visiting speaker would get in a fine Sunday morning church service if he called the congregation "whores." For the rest of his sermon, everybody's eyes would be on him, and they would pay close attention to everything he said.

God often used strong words to His prophets and through His prophets. To Hosea, He said, "Go marry a whore . . . for the country itself has been nothing but a whore . . . ."[4] Through Isaiah, He said, "See how the faithful city has become a harlot . . . ."[5] Through Ezekiel, He said to Jerusalem, "Therefore, you prostitute, hear the word of the Lord!"[6] And through Jeremiah, He said to Israel and Judah, "I have seen your adulteries and your lustful neighings, and the lewdness of your harlotry . . . ."[7] John White calls this "the prophet's whip of cords,"[8] comparing their words to Jesus' words when He drove the moneychangers out of the Temple—and, remember, Jesus said that He spoke what His Father gave Him to speak and did what His Father told Him to do.

John White said, "The Holy Spirit's inspiration of a term like HARLOT, WHORE or PROSTITUTE is designed to sting people into shocked awareness that their sins (whatever those sins might be) enrage God. "[9] But even more jolting is the Holy Spirit's graphic language through Jeremiah, "I will pull up your skirts over your face that your shame may be seen . . . ."[10] God doesn't mince words and He says what He needs to say to get the attention of His people—all He needs are holy prophets like Amos, Hosea, and Jeremiah, who are faithful and bold enough to say and do what God tells them to say and do.

A prophet like Amos may seem like nothing more than an aggressive and arrogant meddler. But when we have a cancer, we want a surgeon who hates cancer fiercely and who is skillful and bold enough to use the surgical knives as he needs to in order to cut out the cancer. Amos, like other God-called prophets, aggressively went after the foul tumor that was damning the nation of Israel. So to awake them from their prosperous apathy, Amos strongly proclaimed to them the clear and certain Word of God.

That Word was their only hope, as Anderson and Freedman pointed out, "In the mounting crisis, . . . Only the Word of God, drastic and devastating as it might be, could avail against the forces both internal and external which threatened the life of the nations and their inhabitants severally."[11]

As we stated in a previous chapter, Amos first addressed the six nations surrounding Israel using an identical pattern to each: God is speaking—there is deep sin—judgment looms—one sin is pinpointed— they are told what will happen to them in their coming judgment The six sins that God pinpoints possess a common characteristic—they are sins that involve brutality or bloodshed, sins of inhumanity. They are sins that even the pagan nations, who did not have the Word of God, knew were wrong.

No doubt, after Amos told of the sins and impending judgment of their wicked neighbors, Israel paid closer attention to him. Then he spoke the Word of God to Judah, Israel's brother to the south:

> This is what the Lord says: "For three sins of Judah, even for four, I will not turn back my wrath. Because they have rejected the law of the Lord and have not kept his decrees, because they have been led astray by false gods, the gods their ancestors followed, I will send fire upon Judah . . . ."[12]

Judah and Israel traced their heritage back to Abraham, and they both had the Word of God, so for Amos to speak so bluntly about their brother-nation undoubtedly created uneasiness in Israel. And Amos speaks the same thing to Judah that he spoke to the six pagan nations. They have great sin, and God will no longer hold back His wrath.

One of their sins was that they abandoned God's law. To have the Word of God is a special privilege, carrying great blessings when obeyed. But Judah foolishly turned aside and followed false gods. Judah replaced God's laws with men's lies, and instead of shaping the surrounding pagan nations with the truth

65

of God's Word (of which they were stewards), they absorbed paganism into their own culture and were refashioned by it into an unholy nation that no longer followed after God. For that, Judah would be judged.

But Amos was not through. He then turned to Israel and proclaimed, "For three sins of Israel, even for four, I will not turn back my wrath."[13] About there, Amos probably gained the attention of a lot of Israelites, and lost the attention of a lot of Israelites—sinning people find it tough to face their sins and the consequential judgment. So God has Amos reel off sin after sin in rapid order—selling the righteous for silver, selling the needy for a pair of sandals, trampling on the heads of the poor, denying justice to the oppressed, father and son using the same prostitute and profaning the holy name of the Lord, lying down beside every altar on garments taken in pledge, drinking the wine of the condemned in the house of God.

It was quite a list. Some in the crowd were probably reeling even before Amos finished. The list pointed to pride, greed, immorality, AND injustice in Israel—and for their sins, the same verdict of judgment as on the pagan nations. Social injustice and inhumanity in Israel received the same judgment as was pronounced earlier on the six pagan nations for their brutalizing injustice and inhumanity. THE SINS OF CIVILIZATION ARE JUDGED MORE HARSHLY THAN THE SINS OF BARBARISM. George Adam Smith said, "The social sins of a civilized and enlightened nation are just as bad as the atrocities of barbarian war and slave-trading and as certain of Divine punishment."[14]

One fundamental reason for the severity of their punishment was that Israel and Judah enjoyed enormous privilege in knowing God and His Word, and therefore had greater responsibility—so their sin carried heavier consequence. Smith makes the point: "The crimes of Israel are greater than those of the heathen;

and that the people's peculiar relation to God means not their security, but their heavier doom. It is then affirmed that Israel's wealth and social life are so sapped by luxury and injustice that the nation must perish."[15] It is as the satirist said of the Romans, "To their crimes they owe their gardens, palaces, stables, and fine old plate."[16] So it was with Israel—and it brought them judgment.

Held to a Higher Standard

The same judgment came down on Israel for the lesser crimes of selling the righteous for silver and trampling on the heads of the poor as came on the pagans for the horrendous crimes of slave-trafficking and ripping open pregnant women, because Israel and Judah had the Law of God and were held to a higher standard. Eventually Israel, and later Judah, began to shed innocent blood as did the pagans. Of Israel's sin, Hosea said, "They break all bounds, and bloodshed follows bloodshed." [17]

This inhumanity defined how far Israel had fallen. For pagan nations to cruelly shed blood was one thing, but for Israel, who knew from Scripture that man is made in the image of God and who had clear commands about the treatment of others, to shed blood was a sin of immensely greater magnitude. In her judgment, there is a strong message for us.

Privilege means higher responsibility, and knowledge means greater accountability. America professes, "In God we trust!" and has had the Word of God daily preached in its midst. God is holding America to its professed word, and He is holding it to a higher, more noble standard than nations that have not so professed. America—and each nation in the West—must understand, as Virginia Corfield wrote, "A nation who covenants with God at its inception, is not only singularly privileged; it is doubly accountable."[18]

Israel did not believe they were accountable for their sins or that God would hold them responsible. Amos tried to get them to understand it. He even went back over the rich heritage and blessings the nation had received from God. He showed them how they had compromised their spiritual leaders—their prophets and their Nazirites. They told the prophets not to prophesy and convinced the Nazirites to drink wine, thereby breaking their vow to God. The Israelites wanted their religious leaders to be like themselves— ignoring sin, only concerned about having a good time, able to hold their wine, just one of the good old boys, just like them. Sometimes God's people even came to think that about God himself, and He had to put them straight.

> These *things* you have done, and I kept silent;
> You thought that I was altogether like you;
> *But* I will rebuke you,
> And set *them* in order before your eyes.[19]

The people of Israel corrupted their godly men and no longer had their guidance, so Israel spiritually fell and began to commit great evil and great injustice— eventually bloodshed followed bloodshed. And God said, "Now then, I will crush you as a cart crushes when loaded with grain."[20]

But even here, in the stern pronouncement of judgment, there is great emotion from the broken heart of the heavenly Father, "Hear this word the Lord has spoken against you, O people of Israel—against the whole family I brought up out of Egypt: 'You only have I chosen of all the families of the earth : . . .'"[21] Love that will not deal strongly with sin is not real love—so the almighty God of the nations, the impartial judge of every one of us, said to Israel, "Therefore I will punish you for all your sins."[22]

Still they do not repent, and Amos must jolt them, so he gets brutally frank with the wealthy women who revel in the luxuries the times offer. He is unsparing of them, and in a phrase fierce with sarcasm calls them "cows of Bashan."[23] (Bashan was a lush pasture, and cows from there were fat and pampered, doing nothing but eating and sleeping all day.) Amos is relentless as he continues his tirade: "You women who oppress the poor and crush the needy and say to your husbands, 'Bring us some drinks!'" Perhaps in their life-styles most of these women never encountered a poor person, but Amos lays the sin of injustice at their feet. Their only concern is for a doting husband to bring them more wine, to wait on them, to keep the good times going.

There is no sin in being prosperous; we will not find that in Amos. But prosperity carries with it extra responsibility and particular dangers—ease and luxury can foster insensitivity. An abundance of things is worthless if we're not right with God. Jesus probed people's attitude toward possessions and most often found them wrong. So we must be extremely careful about what we have and about wanting more. While our nation enjoys the highest standard of living that has existed, with relative luxury in the reach of many, the most tragic injustice of modern times is going on—the shedding of innocent blood. If we've made prosperity the goal of our Christianity, the striving of our faith, and see that alone as God's major blessing—our response to our nation's sins and to our own, can be an indifferent, "Bring us another drink!" It's an important truth that you can hold a coin so close to your eye that you can't see anything else.

Amos told the indifferent women of Israel what their dreadful brutal fate would be when their nation fell: "The Sovereign Lord has sworn by his holiness: 'The time will surely come when you will be taken away with hooks, the last of you with fishhooks. You will each go straight out through breaks in the wall, and you will be cast out toward Harmon,'"[24] He was prophesying the coming overthrow of Israel by the Assyrians.

The Assyrians were cruel. They often punched hooks through prisoners' lips, strung them together and marched them across the desert to Assyria. Amos tells the wealthy, selfish, and self-indulging women of Israel that this is God's punishment for their injustice, for their oppression of the poor and needy.[25]

In the past, the Lord had given many other reproofs and warnings to Israel to bring them back to Him, and now He reminds them of these:

FAMINE: "I gave you empty stomachs in every city and lack of bread in every town . . . ."[26]

DROUGHT: "I also withheld rain from you when the harvest was still three months away . . . ."[27]

CROP FAILURE: "Many times I struck your gardens and vineyards . . . ."[28]

PLAGUES: "I sent plagues among you as I did in Egypt . . . ."[29]

DEFEAT IN BATTLE: "I killed your young men with the sword . . . ."[30]

DISASTERS: "I overthrew some of you as I overthrew Sodom and Gomorrah . . . ."[31]

In this the Lord clearly tells Israel that He was the one who caused the catastrophes; they were neither natural nor came from their enemies—they came from God to chastise His people and warn them to repent: "I gave . . . I withheld . . . I struck . . . I killed . . . I overthrew."

God's Purpose—Repentance

Some people have trouble believing that God would do this. But what was the Lord's purpose? To get them to come back to Him. Five times, from the agonizing heart of the heavenly Father comes the moving words, "Yet you have not returned to me."[32] God's only purpose in these catastrophes was to bring repentance—it was redemptive. That's the major difference between those things that come from God and those things that do not—whatever God brings is always redemptive. And when we respond properly to them, they always bring us back to God or closer to God— they always bring us out from under His wrath and back into His blessings.[33]

What is God saying now to America? In just the past few years we have had "the hurricane of the century" and "the flood of the century." But instead of turning to God, we look up to heaven and whine, "Why us? How could God allow this to happen?"

Why not us? What do we have that so commends us to a holy God that He would withhold disaster from us? In what way are we better than others?

A few people, at least, are beginning to wonder about what is happening to us and casting an eye heavenward. One soap opera actress said, "Fire, riots, floods, and earthquakes. Maybe *somebody* is trying to tell us something." A citizen of Southern California said, "We've had riots, floods, financial troubles, and fires. Do you think *God* means to bring us doom?" But a famous author said, "I don't know why *nature* has turned against us."

Roy Clements commented, "When we read of disasters in our newspapers we are not to dismiss them as unfortunate accidents, nor are we to complain of them as cruel acts of fate. Amos teaches that we are to see in them the rebuking hand of God. Every newspaper headline is a call to repentance for those who have eyes to read it there."[34] But do newspaper headlines drive us to our knees in humility and repentance before God? Of course not!

What about AIDS? We have brought this plague on ourselves. It is transmitted primarily through sinful behavior, whether homosexual or heterosexual sin, or the sharing of drug needles—and even the innocent are now suffering from this plague brought upon our nation and the world by sin. AIDS should jolt us to repent of our extensive, continual sexual perversion and to return to the Lord. Everything that can be shaken is eventually shaken. God is our only secure and safe haven, and He has used both prophets and prominent disasters to call nations and individuals to himself so they will be blessed instead of judged.

Israel refused to listen to the prophet Amos, refused to listen to this man sent by God to chastise and warn them, and so God had a final word for them, "Prepare to meet your God, O Israel."[35] The word "meet," Clements says, is neutral—it can mean meet as enemies on the field of battle, or meet as friends at a meal.[36] Which way the nation met God was up to them, but the summons was firm, "Prepare to meet your God, O Israel." The days of warning are over. You would not listen to God's prophet, Amos, so God himself is now coming to sort out this matter and straighten you out.

God knew they were not ready for such an encounter, so they are to get ready. David Pawson observed, "There is only one way to meet a God like that—and that's by way of unconditional surrender."[37]

God's many warnings to Israel illustrate what Amos had said earlier, that the Lord does not act in judgment without warning, "Surely the Lord does nothing without revealing his plan to his servants the prophets." Then he exclaims in awe, "The lion has roared—who will not fear? The Sovereign Lord has spoken—who can but prophesy?"[38]

God does not surprise any nation or individual with His judgment. If we are surprised, it is not because God has not spoken, it is because we have not listened. When a nation is altogether ripe for ruin, God executes vengeance without any view to their reformation, but until then He will continue to correct them with much longsuffering and forbearance.

We in the West have prospered. We have been blessed by God. But our sins are extensive. We are prideful, immoral, inhumane, ruthless. The daily shedding of innocent blood by the killing of our unborn, and the rampant homosexual perversion in our country, openly expose our nation's newly acquired ruthless and immoral character.

But where are the true prophets who should be telling us this?

Are those who say they are the Lord's spokespersons warning us?

Has the Lion roared?

Or do we have only false voices speaking from the pulpits of our churches?

---

[1] *Insight, Women in Quote*, (Axiom Publishing, Adelaide, Australia, 1990), p. 20.

[2] Billy Graham, *World Aflame*, (Fleming Revell, 1965).

[3] Carl W. Wilson, *Our Dance Has Turned to Death*, (Renewal Publishing), p. 5.

[4] Hosea 1:2 (The Jerusalem Bible).

[5] Isaiah 1:21.

[6] Ezekiel 16:35.

[7] Jeremiah 13:27 (NKJV).

[8] John White, *The Golden Cow*, p. 7.

[9] Ibid., p. 19.

[10] Jeremiah 13:26-27.

[11] Anderson and Freedman, *Hosea*, (Doubleday, 1980), p. 41.

[12] Amos 2:4-5.

[13] Amos 2:6.

[14] George Adam Smith, *Book of the Twelve Prophets*, (Hodder and Stoughton, 1928), p. 139.

[15]Ibid., p. 144.

[16]Juvenal, *Satires, I.*

[17]Hosea 4:2.

[18]Virginia Corfield, *Sow the Wind,* (Provident Press, 1979).

[19]Psalm 50:21 (NKJV).

[20]Amos 2:13.

[21]Amos 3:1-2a.

[22]Amos 3:2b.

[23]Amos 4:1.

[24]Amos 4:2-3.

[25]Amos 4:1.

[26]Amos 4:6.

[27]Amos 4:7.

[28]Amos 4:9.

[29]Amos 4:10.

[30]Amos 4:10.

[31]Amos 4:11.

[32]Amos 4:6, 8-11.

[33]Hebrews 12:10.

[34]Roy Clements, *When God's Patience Runs Out,* (Inter-Varsity, 1988), p. 62.

[35]Amos 4:12.

[36]Roy Clements, *When God's Patience Runs Out,* (Inter-Varsity, 1988), p. 64.

[37]David Pawson, from a sermon on Amos.

[38]Amos 3:8.

6

Well-Established Religion

Just like the secularist, many Christians are 'into' themselves. They do not want authority and they do not want demands made on them . . . . This is . . . decaffeinated Christianity.

John Fleming[1]

A friend told me about a church member he knew years ago who regularly testified in the Sunday evening service. The man had a standard closing, "Twenty years ago, down in the woods, kneeling by an old stump, I got saved," he would say. "And, brothers and sisters, although I'm not makin' much progress, I'm w—e—l—l established!" He said this so often, the other members knew it by heart.

One day some men of the church were cutting winter firewood in the woods. It had rained heavily for several days, and the heavily loaded wagon sank deep into a mud hole. The horses could not free it. One of the men climbed atop the firewood on the hopelessly mired wagon, surveyed the situation, and called down to his testifying friend, in the inflection he knew so well,

"Well, brother, we're not makin' much progress, but we're w—e—l—l established!"

A similar story is told about a young man who got saved in a country church that had been established for years. With the combination of his youth and the flush of his new-born life, he often could not contain his enthusiasm and love of God and Christ and during the meetings would shout things like, "Praise the Lord!— Glory be to God!—Thank you, Jesus!—Amen!— Hallelujah!"

His shouting bothered the pastor and the elders— and the long-time Christians—so much that they finally talked to the young man's father and told him he would have to keep his son quiet, that they could not have such noise in their church. The young man must understand, they said, that they were a respectable and well-established church of long standing. The father agreed with them, and on the way home in the wagon, he told his son what the elders had said. The son promised he would do his best to restrain himself.

Then a few miles from the church, they had to pull off the road to cross a muddy creek because the bridge was out. They got about halfway across the creek and the wagon bogged down and the horses couldn't free it. "Get out, son," the father said, "and see if you can help the horses by pushing the wagon."

The son tried, but the wagon just dug deeper into the creek's muddy bottom. "Can't do it, father," he said, "she won't budge a bit."

The father looked over the side of the wagon and said, "What do you think is the problem, son?"

The son looked down at the wagon wheels sunk deep into the muddy creek bed, then with a grin looked up at his father and said, "Well, father, I think our wagon's gotten established."

Organized religion can quickly get well-established. So well-established, in fact, that many will see the established organization as the only desirable kind of religion, something that's stable and respectable, secure and certain with no surprises—rather than something that's "stuck in the mud."

In the time of Amos, Israel had plenty of religion. They had religious feasts and assemblies, special worship sites at Bethel and Gilgal, and they gave tithes, offerings, and sacrifices. They were very religious and very prosperous. But God hated their religion, as He may well hate ours. The religion of Israel, mixed with the nation's peace and prosperity, was the key ingredient in the sedative that had put the nation to sleep. The enemy of any nation is religion—conservative or evangelical or charismatic—that has mixed the world's values with the Word of God and joins the world in its greed and frolic.

When God sent Amos into the middle of Israel's religious society, He came directly against their injustice:

> You who turn justice into bitterness and cast righteousness to the ground . . . . You trample on the poor and force him to give you grain [the idea is of doing so through a legal veneer] . . . . For I know how many are your offenses and how great your sins [meaning they are terminal]. You oppress the righteous and take bribes and you deprive the poor of justice in the courts.[2]

Israel officially sanctioned injustice against the weak. In the beginning it was only social injustices, but soon "bloodshed followed bloodshed." Their injustice became the same kind of brutal inhumanity practiced by their pagan neighbors. Then in almost a deliberate affront to God, as part of their religious worship, they began to sacrifice their children to the pagan god Molech.[3]

Molech was a hideous-looking idol—half bull, half man, with outstretched arms. Below the arms was a place for a fire. In the orgy of worship of Molech's demon,[4] a roaring fire would be started beneath Molech's arms, and then a live baby would be placed on his arms and burned to death as a sacrifice to him.

Such a barbaric, sacrificial ritual would not be tolerated today by any civilized nation. But we do tolerate the killing of children *before* they're born—out of sight, out of mind!

What's the difference between Israel and the pagan nations sacrificing their living children to Molech's demon and our nation aborting its unborn babies? A very important difference—living children were sacrificed to Molech because *they had value;* our unborn are sacrificed because *they have no value.* Some may object to the word "sacrificed" being used as a synonym for "aborted," but our nation's unborn children are sacrificed as surely as were Israel's living children— their children were sacrificed to appease a demonic idol; ours are sacrificed to appease our selfish desires.

Where were the religious people when this cruel inhumanity was going on? They were active and busy and silent. They were now culturally part of the prospering classes and could not be bothered with such disturbing things; besides, sacrificing babies was now socially acceptable—it was the modern thing to do. So out of the mouths of the worshiping people of God, out of their singing sanctuaries, out in the streets where protest and compassion could be heard, there was only the sound of silence.

Then the Lion roared out of Zion! Roared in language meant to shake the very souls of all who were involved in any *religious ritual of worship,* then or now: "I hate, I despise your religious feasts; I cannot stand your assemblies. Even though you bring me burnt offerings and grain offerings, I will not accept them.

Though you bring choice fellowship offerings, I will have no regard for them. Away with the noise of your songs! I will not listen to the music of your harps."[5] They had abounding worship that they totally enjoyed and were surrounded by abounding sin that they totally ignored.

Theologian Karl Barth put God's words in a modern setting: "I hate, I despise your lectures and seminars, your sermons, addresses, and Bible studies, and I take no delight in your discussions, meetings and conventions."[6]

Modern church life is packed with Sunday services, seminars, spiritual celebrations, retreats, special days, city-wide campaigns, camps. Read the brochures, read the magazines. Are these meaningless to God, nothing but religious activities we busily and blithely practice while evil multiplies around us and judgment looms? Could it be that while we delightedly skip from one happy spiritual event to the other, enjoying with abandon all the uplift, renewal, and blessing they appear to bring, God is saying, "I hate, I despise, I cannot stand them?"

Can we afford to ignore this question?

And what about our hymns, our choirs, our spiritual songs, our dancing, our clapping, our shouting—those things we so much enjoy listening to or doing when we "worship?" Could God be saying, "Away with the noise . . . I will not listen . . . "? Could that be possible? Could God not enjoy what we enjoy? Could we be that deceived? Israel was. Others have been. Pastors and worship leaders should set aside their personal feelings and desires—if it is possible for them to do so—and humble themselves and truly seek the Lord for the answer to this question.

God was so fed up with Israel's well-established but sin-ignoring religion, that He mocked it, "'Go to Bethel and sin; go to Gilgal and sin yet more. Bring your sacrifices every morning, your tithes every three years. Burn leavened bread as a thank offering and brag about your freewill offerings—boast about them, you Israelites, for this is what you love to do,' declares the Sovereign Lord."[7] For a lot of Christians today, those Words of God strike close to home.

Why does the Lord abhor so much of what we consider to be good, even Spirit-led and anointed, religious activities?

Well, what did the Lord want from Israel, from His chosen people? What could they have done that would have pleased Him? "But let justice roll on like a river, righteousness like a never-failing stream!"[8]

There's the answer. Justice. Righteousness. That's what the Lord is looking for in His people—their demonstration of His character in them! From Israel, God wanted justice and righteousness pouring abundantly from them at all times.[9] Such things would bless and save the nation of Israel, and such things will bless and save our nation—or any nation of the West.

The Lord wants worship—whether Protestant or Catholic, liturgical or non-liturgical, evangelical, fundamental, Pentecostal, or charismatic—THAT FOCUSES ON *KNOWING* HIM MORE.[10] "Seek *me* and live!"[11] The people who *know* God care deeply about the things that God cares about.

When we have no heart or desire to truly *know* God, and no concern about injustice and unrighteousness, God despises our multitude of religious events, our rituals, our kneeling at altars, our lifting our hands in praise. They are empty words and sounds before Him, rattling noises that have no meaning to Him. He turns His ear away and does not hear. Unless we are spiritually dead and do not know it, surely we can feel the heat of His displeasure at our self-deceived worship.

Worship That Pleases God

True worship comes out of a heart that wants to please God, not to please self. And true worship, in turn, motivates the worshiper to do those things that please God—such as having compassion, acting justly, and living righteously. These are both a result and a sign of true worship. Otherwise, worship is nothing more than religious play, something that the person enjoys doing and has convinced himself or herself that God enjoys it. True worshipers, however, care first and foremost about what the heart of God cares about, and they will use their hands, feet, and voices to bring about what He cares about.

Amos was not the only prophet God used to speak strongly to His people. The prophet Micah said, "And what does the Lord require of you? To act justly and to love mercy and to walk humbly with your God."[12] And Isaiah, the great prophet to Judah, used the same strong language to gave God's opinion of the worship He hates:

> When you come to appear before me, who has asked this of you, this trampling of my courts? Stop bringing meaningless offerings! Your incense is detestable to me. New Moons, Sabbaths and convocations—I cannot bear your evil assemblies. Your New Moon festivals and your appointed feasts my soul hates. They have become a burden to me; I am weary of bearing them. When you spread out your hands in prayer, I will hide my eyes from you; even if you offer many prayers, I will not listen. Your hands are full of blood; wash and make yourselves clean. Take your evil deeds out of my sight! Stop doing wrong, learn to do right! Seek justice, encourage the oppressed. Defend the cause of the fatherless, plead the case of the widow.[13]

Later Isaiah added, "See how the faithful city has become a harlot! She once was full of justice; righteousness used to dwell in her—but now murderers! . . . THEY DO NOT DEFEND THE CAUSE OF THE FATHERLESS; THE WIDOW'S CASE DOES NOT COME BEFORE THEM"[14] (Emphasis mine).

To this we should add our Lord's statement, "And whoever welcomes a little child like this in my name welcomes me." No matter what our personal opinion is of capital punishment, what the Lord says next should give us pause: "But if anyone causes one of these little ones who believe in me to sin, it would be better for him to have a large millstone hung around his neck and to be drowned in the depths of the sea. Woe to the world because of the things that cause people to sin!"[15]

Then there is this statement from James: "Religion that God our Father accepts as pure and faultless is this: to look after orphans and widows in their distress and to keep oneself from being polluted by the world."[16]

As the Body of God's Son, we dare not ignore the certainty of what pleases His Father and our Father in religion and in worship.

Religion that is truly spiritual—in worship and in service—is never a private affair. Modern religion, however, tries to make it private by carefully keeping its professions and activities within church and parish, and within the proper bounds that society's good manners dictate. But that kind of wishy-washy Christian attitude would have been unthinkable and abominable to Madame Guyon, John Wesley, George Whitefield, Jonathan Edwards, David Brainerd, Hudson Taylor, William Wilberforce, Charles Finney, John "Praying" Hyde, Amy Carmichael, and a multitude of others in the great and dynamic history of the Church.

As a Christian preacher, Finney spoke out uncompromisingly against slavery in America, which was the watershed injustice of his day in the same way that the killing of the unborn is now. After a newspaper report that whites and blacks would be allowed to sit together in Finney's Broadway Tabernacle when its construction was completed, irate citizens set the building on fire and the firemen refused to put out the blaze. Finney often tied injustice and revivals tightly together and once said, "Revivals are hindered when ministers and churches take the wrong ground in regard to questions of human rights." He went on:

> It is doubtless true, that one of the reasons for the low state of religion at the present time is that many Churches have taken the wrong side on the subject of slavery, and have suffered prejudice to prevail over principle, and have feared to call this abomination by its true name.[17]

Today, we have physicians tearing the unborn piece by piece from the womb with suction or forceps, or by injecting chemicals into them to kill them—and often leaving them unattended on a table to die if they survive—all without even a pain-killing injection. This is an inhumanity as brutal and as calloused as any barbarism that has ever been practiced by pagans.

But our guilt is multiplied immeasurably by the callous deceptions that tell our public conscience it is proper and moral to choose such violence. The Scriptures clearly tell us that the bloody and cruel injustice we are waging against our unborn is the same kind of injustice that brought God's wrath upon Israel and the pagan nations. The Israel that was in the days of Amos ceased to exist. So did the six neighboring nations. Will ours? If God judged and punished them, will He not do the same to us?

Yet what is the Church doing in such a crucial moment? Is it doing what Israel was when Amos appeared—enjoying religious celebrations, caught up in its worship, its services, conferences, camps and seminars? Is it basking in its healing and prosperity messages—healthy, wealthy, and not so wise?

God hates religion that is not concerned about sin, as we can see in His treatment of Israel. National iniquity sent Israel over the precipice. Will it send us over as well? Before it does, what can we do to hold back the judgment of God? The Holy Spirit clearly tells us through the prophet Joel:

> Blow the trumpet in Zion, declare a holy fast, call a sacred assembly. Gather the people, consecrate the assembly; bring together the elders, gather the children, those nursing at the breast. Let the bridegroom leave his room and the bride her chamber. Let the priests, who minister before the Lord, weep between the temple porch and the altar. Let them say, "Spare your people, O Lord."[18]

When Amos came with God's rebuking words to Israel, their well-established political and religious leaders were at ease and loving their fine life-styles and prosperity. They were under the illusion that because they personally were doing so well, the nation was strong and safe. They were a stone's throw from judgment and did not know it—or did not care. It is typical of people—and especially religious leaders—to deny coming judgment, or at least think of it as far off, while all around them their nation continues in the sin that is bringing it. As Roy Clements says, "Men and women always prefer a soothing lie than a disturbing truth."[19]

Israel's leaders had no sense of need, no conviction to repent, so they did not grieve over their nation's moral ruin that was raging all around them. Rather than setting a moral example, they were busy living their lives of ease, unconcerned about the spiritual state of their nation, and blind to the signs and warnings of

God that would have been so easy to see if they had the spiritual eyes with which to see them.

And what of now? Who will lead our nation and the nations of the West to grieve over the moral ruin of our society? Will its political leaders? Will the Church?

Trusting in Deceptive Words

Israel's problem was that it was a nation that had been misled spiritually by false prophets. These false preachers proclaimed optimistic messages that ignored the nation's sin as if they would not have to answer to God for it. They taught the people that "the day of the Lord" was going to bring great blessings and prosperity on them, when the Word of God clearly said that it would be a day before God of judgment, a day on which they would have to give account to God for their sins. These false teachers centered on the nation's privileged heritage, instead of on obedience to God's Word, and taught that the nation's status made them exempt from judgment. They tickled the people's ears, and the people rewarded them for their pleasant words and joyful news of guaranteed blessings from God on "the day of the Lord" no matter what kind of lives they lived.

Judah later had the same delusion, but with an added dimension. The Temple was at Jerusalem and their false prophets taught them that they would always be safe no matter what happened to anyone else—all they had to do was confess correctly and they had nothing to worry about. So Judah, blindly relying on what the false prophets said and their status as the people of God, glibly recited, "This is the temple of the Lord, the temple of the Lord, the temple of the Lord!"[20]? They had been told that a positive confession like that would keep them safe from judgment, regardless of

their sins. Rather than check the Word of God themselves, they chose to believe the false prophets. They
probably felt better that way. And, after all, God would
not harm Jerusalem where His Temple was. So they
went merrily on their way, occasionally going into the
house of the Lord to stand before Him and say, "We
are safe—safe to do all these detestable things."[21]

Through Jeremiah, the Lord was searing in His
rebuke of the sinning nation, and bluntly told them they
were trusting "in deceptive words." Then He said to
them, "Reform your ways and your actions, and I will
let you live in this place," and, "Do not oppress the alien,
the fatherless or the widow and do not shed innocent
blood in this place."[22]

Jeremiah then told Judah to go to Shiloh, where God
had once put His Name, and see there what He had
done when the people were wicked. In the first book
of Samuel, we have the account of the sordid evil and
God's devastating judgment. Eli's daughter-in-law, who
gave birth to a son during that tragic time, described the
nation's resultant spiritual condition in the name she
gave her newborn: "Then she named the child Ichabod,
saying, 'The glory has departed from Israel!' because the
ark of God had been captured and because of her father-
in-law and her husband."[23]

Israel and Judah believed the lie that they could sin
and carry right on with their religious activities in God's
house. As George Adam Smith said, Israel "with pagan
folly . . . believed that the smoke of their burnt-offerings
went up to heaven and flattered the nostril of Deity."[24]
They thought they were safe, so they had little place for
rebuke or holy living, no place for sin or judgment, and
no thought that God was dishonored and displeased.
They believed only what made them feel good, only
what made them spiritually comfortable and satisfied,
even though they had been warned often of imminent
judgment. That deadly spiritual condition is very hard
to dislodge.

Israel's compromised spiritual outlook gave them a rosy, cozy view of the future—the day of the Lord would come and everything would be great for them. This is the tragic fruit of deceptive, positive-only words. As John Marsh said about Israel, "A true prophet had to burst this blasphemous bubble."[25] So God's true prophet, Amos, ripped into that deadly false security with stinging words:

> Woe to you who desire the day of the LORD!
> For what good *is* the day of the LORD to you?
> It *will be* darkness, and not light.
> It *will be* as though a man fled from a lion,
> And a bear met him!
> Or *as though* he went into the house,
> Leaned his hand on the wall,
> And a serpent bit him!
> *Is* not the day of the Lord darkness, and not light?
> *Is it not* very dark, with no brightness in it?[26]

Earlier Amos had said, "Seek good, not evil, that you may live. Then the Lord God Almighty will be with you, just as you say he is."[27]

The day of the Lord is a coin with two sides—a day of redemption, blessing, and vindication for the people of God, and a day of accounting and judgment for those opposed to God. On the one hand, light and rejoicing—on the other, darkness and terror. Israel was so caught up with the light and rejoicing that they ignored what the prophets proclaimed repeatedly: "Judgment always begins with the people of God."[28] God will not permit His people to do those things for which He will justly judge the world.

Sadly, today's unbalanced teachings about the future keep Christians away from impacting their world with the Gospel of Christ. In some places Christians are taught that things are so bad there is no use trying to do anything—and in other places they are taught that we are doing so well there is no need to be concerned. A healthy, balanced view of the future, however, will make a Christian center on Christ and His redemptive work, joyfully look forward to His return, boldly declare the coming judgment, and confront our world wherever it is morally wrong. A balanced view will produce holiness and hope in us.

Roy Clements stressed, "The Bible does not tell us about the end of the world merely to satisfy our curiosity. The primary function of future prophecy is to galvanize us into moral action here and now. God did not send prophets to Israel to amuse their bored minds or to soothe their anxious hearts. He sent them to turn people to repentance. 'The day of the Lord is coming. Be different, change, get ready.' That was their message."[29]

The language of Amos was as foreboding as a funeral dirge. At one point, he even expressed such a lament: "Fallen is Virgin Israel, never to rise again, deserted in her own land, with no one to lift her up."[30]

Here again is the great heart of the heavenly Father. It is as if He is standing over the casket of the "virgin," Israel, who had so much potential and for whom He had so many great dreams, but who fell and died.

Amos probably spoke the elegy during one of Israel's festivals. The contrast punctuated the message. Amid the hilarity, the dancing, the mirth, the fun, Amos preached their funeral—they were in a moral crisis, sinning wantonly, and as good as dead.

For the moment, Israel enjoyed the good life; but soon a terrible day of devastation would come, and with it the sobering recognition that God had brought it about just as He said He would through His prophet. Israel would then be afraid to even speak the Lord's name lest they use it wrong and a new torrent of judgment be released.[31]

Earlier God had said to them, "seek me and live."[32]

If they did, He would not bring judgment against them. There was nothing complicated about their redemption, God had already told them what they must do:

> Seek good and not evil,
> That you may live;
> So the Lord God of hosts will be with you,
> As you have spoken.
> Hate evil, love good;
> Establish justice in the gate.
> It may be that the Lord God of hosts
> Will be gracious to the remnant of Joseph.[33]

If they did not repent, however, their punishment was sure and certain—not a matter of whether, just a matter of when—for God told them, "I abhor the pride of Jacob and detest his fortresses; I will deliver up the city and everything in it. . . . For the Lord has given the command, and he will smash the great house into pieces and the small house into bits. . . . For the Lord God Almighty declares 'I will stir up a nation against you, O house of Israel, that will oppress you all the way from Lebo Hamath to the valley of the Arabah.'"[34]

But did anyone listen? Did anyone pay attention to Amos? Or Hosea? No. But what could be expected when the nation's laws, politics, and religion all sanctioned great sin—when the needy were exploited in the courts and the pious were too preoccupied with their good-time activities to do or say anything? Both the national leaders and the spiritual leaders were too busy doing their own thing to lead the people back to God.

So judgment came.

Is there a lesson here for us? For our members of legislatures and parliaments? For our judges? For our community leaders? For our businessmen and women? For our pastors, our ministers, our priests, our evangelists?

Whatever part of the Body of Christ we belong to—
is our religion "established" or prophetic?

As a matter of highest urgency, we need to stop our
religious play and diversions and weigh deeply the
absolute immensity of our nation's sins. We must stop
all our excuse-making, all our rhetoric and ration-
alizations, and face the extent of how self-centered,
prideful, and ruthless we and our nation have become.
In whatever way we sin, we do so against the goodness
of God that should lead us to repentance.[35]

We *must* repent. If we do not repent, it is not then
a matter of whether judgment will come, just when it
will come. If we do not repent, then we will deserve
the fate that is now casting its shadow over our nation.

Israel wouldn't repent.

Let's pray that we will.

And let's pray that the Church will lead the way.

---

[1]John Fleming, *Religious Decline and Its Consequences,* (La Trobe University, Bundoora, Vic, Australia), p. 12.

[2]Amos 5:7, 11-12.

[3]Jeremiah 32:35.

[4]1 Corinthians 10:19-21.

[5]Amos 5:21-23.

[6]Karl Barth, *The Twelve Prophets, Volume I,* (Saint Andrew Press, Edinburgh), p. 165.

[7]Amos 4:4-5.

[8]Amos 5:24.

[9]John 7:38.

[10]Philippians 3:10.

[11]Amos 5:4.

[12]Micah 6:8.

[13]Isaiah 1:12-17.

[14]Isaiah 1:21-23b.

[15]Matthew 18:5-7a.

[16]James 1:27.

[17]Charles G. Finney, *Revivals of Religion,* (Revell), pp. 325, 327.

[18]Joel 2:15-17.

[19]Roy Clements, *When God's Patience Runs Out,* (Inter-Varsity, 1988), p. 111.

[20]Jeremiah 7:4b.

[21]Jeremiah 7:10b.

[22]From Jeremiah 7:3-8.

[23]1 Samuel 4:21 (NKJV).

[24]George Adam Smith, *The Twelve Prophets,* (Hodder and Stoughton, 1928), p. 174.

[25]John Marsh, *Amos,* (SCM Press, London, 1959), p. 56.

[26]Amos 5:18-20 (NKJV).

[27]Amos 5:14.

[28]1 Peter 4:17 (NKJV).

[29]Roy Clements, *When God's Patience Runs Out,* (Inter-Varsity, 1988), p. 92.

[30]Amos 5:2.

[31]Amos 6:9-10.

[32]Amos 5:4.

[33]Amos 5:14-15 (NKJV).

[34]Amos 6:8-14.

[35]Romans 2:4.

7

False Prophets

It is a remarkable fact that some of the bitterest
enemies who ever confronted the Old Testament
prophets were not priests and worshippers of Baal,
but other prophets of Yahweh.

David Payne[1]

A children's Sunday school class decided to play
church, with ministers, ushers, communion, choir,
organist, and all. After a while they tired of playing
the game and decided to change it. One boy said, "I
know, let's play Jesus." The other children asked him
how to play that game.

He replied, "I'll play Jesus, and the rest of you be
mean to me, call me names, spit on me, hit me, and then
tie me to a tree and pretend you're crucifying me."
They all agreed that it sounded like a fun game.

But after being banged around quite roughly and
spit on several times, the boy playing Jesus decided it
wasn't so much fun after all. He didn't really want any
more of that, so he stopped everything and said, "Let's
not play Jesus any more. Let's go back to playing
church!"

Depending on where we are in our Christianity, that kind of story can make us smile and yell "OUCH!" at the same time.

Those of us in the ministry spend our lives doing religious things. And we can get very good at it— sometimes too good, until the religious activity becomes the end in itself. When that happens, sometimes instead of fulfilling the mandate of the high calling of ministry and the privilege of serving Christ, we end up—well—playing church.

When that happens, we become false ministers— and false prophets. Those around us may not pick up on it for a long time, but deep within ourselves we know what has happened to us. That is, of course, unless we have gotten better at self-deception than we are at self-analysis. Nevertheless, once we are no longer fulfilling the true call of Christ, no longer preaching the true Gospel of Christ, the size of our ministry, our influence, our position, our public exposure in the media, our travels, and our books are all without worth—they are nothing more than religious trappings, the decorated cover of a Bible that has no pages.

We are called by Christ to be shepherds of local churches, of our communities, and of our nation. We are to find pasture and water for the sheep in our care, see after their various spiritual and material needs, watch over their souls, and guard them from the wolves that come prowling out of the darkness. Today, however, we often make room among our flocks for the wolves and adjust the food we feed so that the wolves will be fed and grow as fat and healthy as our sheep— even if they remain wolves. But true shepherds don't invite wolves into their flock, they either run them off or kill them.

In the early 1980s, there were two questions that I especially grappled with. At the time they seemed very difficult to answer. The first question was: *In sanctioning the killing of our unborn today, could we be doing the same kind of thing that brought judgment on Old Testament Israel and Judah when they shed innocent blood?*

The second question came from trying to answer the first question: *Is it possible for a minister who accepts the Bible as the Word of God, who believes Christ is our only Savior and Lord, who believes the essentials of Christianity, to be what the Bible would call a "false prophet?"*

The answer to the first question resulted in my book *Cry of the Innocents.*[2] But I continued to wrestle intellectually and spiritually with the second question, a wrestling that now surprises me.

Perhaps my struggle was caused in part by the fact that in the early 1980s, the Christian community in America was dominated by a lavish style of Christianity. There were massive television ministries that were led by larger-than-life personalities who enjoyed luxurious life-styles and were accorded great celebrity. There was an extensive emphasis on Christian health and wealth, and many ministries were teaching, or strongly implying, that as a Christian you had a Christ-bought right to great material benefits—which would be yours if you learned how to believe correctly—have faith, that is. Also, "entrepreneurial pastors," those who developed mega-churches and oversaw large staffs and massive budgets, had started to appear on the Christian stage.

It was in this spiritual climate that I was trying to find a scriptural answer to my question as to whether a minister of the Gospel of Christ could be what the Scriptures called a "false prophet." I knew that the Lord was clear in His warning: "Beware of false prophets, who come to you in sheep's clothing, but inwardly they are ravenous wolves."[3] But I had always put them outside the Church in a cult, or as some eccentric who claimed he was the Messiah. On closer reading of the Lord's warning, however, I saw that He doesn't put false prophets *outside* the Church, but *in* the Church—they "come to you in *sheep's* clothing."

In addition, there is that disturbing passage from the Sermon on the Mount: "Many will say to me on that day, 'Lord, Lord, did we not prophesy in your name, and in your name drive out demons and perform many miracles?'" This puts this group inside the Church as professed followers and also points to a great need for caution on the part of Pentecostals and charismatics who are the main workers of deliverance and miracles and the gift of prophecy.[4]

Jesus continued, "Then I will tell them plainly, 'I never knew you. Away from me, you evildoers!'"[5] This is an uncompromising final judgment on a false ministry, which makes it a matter of great concern to all of us. The Lord also said, "Not everyone who says to me, 'Lord, Lord,' will enter the kingdom of heaven, but only he who does the will of my Father who is in heaven."[6]

Just before the Apostle Paul left the elders at Ephesus to sail to Jerusalem, he exhorted them to "Keep watch over yourselves and all the flock . . . ." He then cautioned them about a spiritual danger that would come not from outside the Church, but from inside: "I know that after I leave, savage wolves will come in among you and will not spare the flock. Even from your own number men will arise and distort the truth in order to draw away disciples after them. So be on your guard!"[7]

To find the answer to the question of whether a minister of the Gospel could become what the Bible would define as a false prophet, I also studied Amos and Hosea, the last writing prophets to the Northern Kingdom of Israel. This, in turn, led me to study the writings of several other Old Testament prophets such as Ezekiel and Jeremiah.

Each of the prophets, Amos, Hosea, Ezekiel, and

Jeremiah, had an urgent, pivotal message for their nation—a message that, if heeded, would bring restoration and blessing. When the sin of these nations reached a crucial point and they headed toward their end in judgment, God in His loving care sent these prophets to warn them and call them back to himself. Their messages contained forceful and bold exposure of sin, and strong repeated warnings of forthcoming judgment unless there was repentance. But the nations did not listen and would not listen. In every case, they had nothing but caustic scorn for both the message and the messenger.

Why didn't the nations listen?

We could say that it was because they were too settled in their prosperity, too materialistic, and that the messages upset their life-styles. That would partially be true. We could also say that it was because they were so violent and immoral, even amoral. That would also partially be true. To those reasons we could add that it was because they had an active but distracted religion. Again, partially true. But even together, these answers don't add up to the real reason that they did not listen to God's prophets. We can only find that reason by looking at where the Lord himself placed the responsibility for both the sin and the inattention of the people.

He placed that terrible blame at the feet of false prophets—those prophets who were charged with teaching the people the Word of God, or leading the people spiritually, but who did not faithfully proclaim all *of God's Word.*

Now God judged the nations for their sins; they *were* guilty of committing them and they must be punished. But it was because of the false prophets that the nations were complacent in their sins, were not convicted about them, easily continued to sin, and remained unconcerned about any resulting judgment. In fact, Israel and Judah stayed unconcerned about judgment because the false prophets put a continual emphasis on their national heritage and status, so the two nations simply would not believe that God would judge them. God pointedly laid the blame for Jerusalem's fall to the false prophets in language that should cause preachers to tremble: "The visions of your prophets were false and worthless; they did not expose your sin to ward off your captivity. The oracles they gave you were false and misleading."[8]

F. C. Cook said of the time of Jeremiah:

> The false prophets assured the people of prosperity and deliverance. Their purpose was gain and popularity. The result for the people was being removed from the land—judgment. . . . The false prophets in his days were so numerous and influential as to counteract and almost nullify the influence of the true prophet. . . . But the secret of their power was MY PEOPLE LOVE TO HAVE IT SO (Jeremiah 5:31)[9] (Emphasis mine).

The messages of the false prophets focused so continuously on positive and optimistic themes—"peace, peace"—and spoke so often of prosperity that Israel and Judah simply accepted by default the perilous delusion that the Lord would not deal with their sin, that He would not judge them. The people had itching ears and the false prophets tickled them. Today their books and tapes would sell well. But God himself does not deal lightly with such matters. In the Scriptures, His most trenchant and severe statements are those against false prophets.

Up to this time in my search, however, I still had not been able to determine to my satisfaction whether a minister of the Gospel today could be so defined. The question continued to trouble me, but I felt that I was on dangerous ground and wanted to move cautiously and not make any rash decisions. In Church history, rash and unbalanced statements have often been made concerning who was or was not true, with accusations flagrantly thrown at servants of the Lord. But I couldn't leave the question alone just because of my concerns; I had to have an answer.

I came to realize that the question had to be redirected if I was going to get anywhere. I was too concerned about those *outside* the Church who might or might not be false. I needed to start by being concerned about the ones *in* the Church—especially *me*. Don't worry about seeing the mote in someone else's eye, I told myself, look into your own eye to see if there's a mote.

So my question became, *Could I—as someone who believes he's a committed minister of the Gospel, and who accepts the Scriptures as the inspired Word of God and Christ as the only Savior and Lord—be defined as a false prophet?* Or, at minimum, could I have done what a false prophet does? (This would be a bit better than the first question.)

Asking these questions about myself shook me.

I thought about my ministry, sermons, programs, and the things I've written. I tried to be as objective and fair as possible in my self-evaluation. My conclusion was that most of my ministry had been correct. But I also concluded that at times, perhaps unthinking and even well-intentioned, I had done what a false prophet does.

If I had, pleading before God that I had been well-intentioned or meant well was no defense, nor was pleading that I had been uninformed, naive, green, mostly right, or that I came close—even though I might have been all of these. That was not enough! God places profound priority on His ministers getting His message RIGHT, and He accepts no alibis! CLOSE only counts in horseshoes, hand grenades, and haircuts. Spiritual and moral issues are too crucial, the destiny and care of immortal souls too consequential, and the health and direction of society too pivotal, for us to be inaccurate *for any reason* when delivering God's message. The lawyer's mistakes go to jail, the doctor's mistakes go to the cemetery, but the minister's mistakes go to hell!

This means, of course, that as ministers we'd better be certain of the scriptural truth of what we are teaching as we look closely at just what a false prophet is and does.

There are two kinds of false prophets mentioned in the Scriptures. The first are those who followed idols, such as the ones Elijah encountered on Mt. Carmel. In a strict sense they were not called "false" prophets, simply prophets of idols like Baal or Asherah,[10] but that made them false. The second were those who professed Jehovah—they were within the recognized religious community of either the Old Testament Hebrews or the New Testament Church and knew the Scriptures well.

About false prophets in the Scriptures, Lynn Buzzard said, "Within the biblical tradition there were a host of prophets, even prophet bands, and most were unfaithful, false and political soothsayers. They were the culturally seduced, the fair-haired boys of the establishment, the assurers of victory."[11]

It is these second ones that we want to look at.

We'll examine first the marks of a *false ministry*, which is what we'll call it, as given in the Scriptures.

A False Ministry Develops an "Amaziah" Spirit

Amaziah was the priest at Bethel who told Amos to leave the country and go back to Judah.[12] Amaziah represented the *established religion* in Bethel. In his case, he was a priest for Jeroboam in the state church of Israel and enjoyed the considerable prestige and comfortable perks that the prosperous nation accorded a man in his position as head of the established religion.

An *established religion* can be any religious system or religious group, large or small. Most of us think of the Amaziah spirit as the other minister's problem and are exceedingly blind to it in ourselves. But there are Protestant and Catholic Amaziahs; and there are evangelical, Pentecostal and charismatic Amaziahs— who are the most vulnerable because they don't think they are vulnerable. As soon as any of us gets established in ministry in whatever way, and there exists for us a vested interest in perpetuating what we are doing or building, the Amaziah spirit becomes a big temptation. The Amaziah spirit particularly tempts the advocates of some new teaching or doctrinal fad to establish a new ministry separate from the historical mainline church which doesn't teach the "new revelation." Amaziahs can put out books and tapes and have lavish ministries. Amaziahs get so good at the activity of ministry that they think they are just fine and on track. But, eventually, Amaziahs lose the tender heart after God, humility, and the sheer joy of pleasing and working for the Lord for the sake of the Lord.

Under normal church conditions, the Amaziah spirit stays well-hidden beneath a hypocritical facade of spirituality until true prophets like Amos show up. Amos made Amaziah uncomfortable. No doubt Amos was seen as one of those religious fanatics that Amaziahs have had to put up with throughout Church history.

Amaziah had told King Jeroboam, untruthfully, that Amos was raising a conspiracy against the king, and Amaziah said, "The land cannot bear all his words."[13] Amaziahs miss the real Word of God. What Amos was saying, Amaziah should have been saying—the nation is sinning and headed toward judgment.

Yet here was this man of the cloth confronting the prophet of God and telling him, "Get out!" Perhaps

Amaziah had been so compromised by prosperity that he figured that anyone showing up in Israel might just be there to pick up some of the country's plenty and cut into his share. "Go back to the land of Judah," he told Amos. "Earn your bread there and do your prophesying there." Then he defended Bethel's established religion: "Don't prophesy anymore at Bethel, because this is the king's sanctuary and the temple of the kingdom."[14]

What blindness! Here was the nation of Israel in peril, and before Amaziah stood a man with the one message that, if heeded, would save it. Yet, incredibly, Amaziah's first concern was to protect his religious turf. It was like telling someone with a medical cure for cancer to "Get out!" because you're making money by laying hands on cancer victims.

No wonder the nation didn't listen to Amos, nor to Hosea. No wonder they didn't repent. The head of the established religion, Amaziah, kept them from it. Amaziah—and all of Israel's Amaziahs—was so filled with the spirit of that thriving age, so comfortable in the perks of prosperity, and so blinded to the enormous iniquity of his country, that he let Israel continue its contented gaiety straight into judgment.

Amaziah was Israel's real enemy.

Amaziahs are every nation's real enemy.

There are important questions here for us. In America and the nations of the West today—nations in which our cups of iniquity are rapidly filling and in which gross perversion and bloody injustice are openly permitted—do we have multitudes of Amaziahs who are comfortable in their established ministries, at ease in their prosperity, and deliberately have their eyes closed to evil and judgment and the need for national repentance? Can it be that modern Amaziahs are allowing America to plunge blindly ahead into damnation, while they do all they can to silence any modern Amos that may come into their established territory?

This is a question that I must—I repeat, I MUST!—critically ask about myself: "Am I now, or have I ever been, an Amaziah?"

The Scriptures demand that each minister ask this question of himself or herself. The work we do is too critical to the well being of the eternal souls of countless millions, and to the well being of our nation, to ignore the very real possibility that somewhere in us may dwell tentacles of the Amaziah spirit.

In a False Ministry, Men and Women Do Not Turn From Wickedness

Jesus said that false prophets will be recognized by their fruit.[15] One fruit of a false ministry is that people do not turn from their evil ways as they do in a true ministry. Of false prophets, Jeremiah said, "They strengthen the hands of evildoers, so that no one turns from his wickedness . . . . because from the prophets of Jerusalem ungodliness has spread throughout the land."[16] God's bottom-line evaluation for any of our ministries is, DO MEN AND WOMEN TURN FROM EVIL?

One of western society's dominant philosophies is pragmatism—what works is what is good—especially in America, and many churches fall prey to this mind set. They suppose that if something produces what churches are supposed to produce today according to society's measure of success—a crowd, commitments, goals, excitement, money, growth—it's good, so let's have lots of it.

One consequence of such an attitude is that it may not be spiritual life that impels the church, but pragmatic, success-producing activities and programs. The pastor, evangelist, church leader, or worker whom we might regard as successful today, may or may not be the most godly among us; but it is a strong possibility he or she could be the most success-producing. In fact, a minister who has once satisfied the basic spiritual requirements for ordination in his denomination, can remain on that spiritual level for his entire ministry, and still be regarded as spiritually successful because he learns how to work prag-matically, learns how to produce success according to society's measurements. A *successful* ministry has become the aim rather than a *faithful* ministry—and the two words are not necessarily synonymous.

Now most ministers would not want to admit to being so crass as to put success ahead of faithfulness. The point is, however, that pragmatic, false standards can, and have, become the criteria for success—and thus the environment for false ministry is created and, worse, perpetuated.

So, for myself, I must allow the penetrating voice of God to ask the most important question about every aspect of my ministry: DO THE PEOPLE TO WHOM I MINISTER FORSAKE SIN? Not is there a large attendance, many adherents, many decisions, but *do men and women forsake sin, do they give it up, do they turn from their wicked ways and lead righteous lives?* The main fruit of a true ministry of any size will be men and women turning from wickedness. By contrast, a false ministry allows men and women to remain comfortable in their sin, unrepentant and deceived about the consequences.

A False Ministry Does Not Warn About Judgment, but Emphasizes "Peaceful" Themes

Twice Jeremiah lamented, "Prophets and priests alike, all practice deceit. They dress the wound of my people as though it were not serious. 'Peace, peace,' they say, when there is no peace."[17] And later he said, "Do not listen to what the prophets are prophesying to you; they fill you with false hopes . . . . They keep saying to those who despise me, 'The Lord says: You will have peace.'"[18]

The promise of peace by those false prophets was a naked lie, a devastating lie, a whitewash of sin. God was very clear in telling of the dreadful days ahead for the nation: "See, the storm of the Lord will burst out in wrath, a whirlwind swirling down on the heads of the wicked. The anger of the Lord will not turn back until he fully accomplishes the purposes of his heart."[19]

The dominating scandal of a false ministry is that it lies by what it leaves out, by what it omits, by what it doesn't say. The false prophets in Jeremiah's day omitted what the people really needed to know, that they were going to face judgment. It is a false kindness, a spurious love, that will not warn of coming judgment. A false ministry ignores and leaves out of its teachings how heinous sin is to God, how certain sin brings judgment, and the absolute necessity of repentance.

A false prophet willfully does not examine whether his nation is near collapse because of its great sin, nor considers that the disease of wanton evil in the nation is a fatal one. False prophets are charlatans and preach a charlatan message that treats cancers with Band-Aids. They bandage "the wound of my people as though it were not serious" by their unbalanced, sunny focus. F. C. Cook says, "It is a criterion of false teaching that it lightens the yoke or burden or responsibility of God's law—what God requires—removes God's fear from the conscience, and leaves man to his own nature; man does what he wants. And with this, man is only to ready to be content."[20]

Cook further emphasizes that the false prophets drew their inspiration from the idolatry around them in their society. In today's society, we have a humanistic idolatry that dominates a very self-absorbed, hedonistic generation that is focused on concerns of self, personal needs, comforts, happiness, and pleasures. The language of sin has been replaced with psychological jargon. Today we want our religion to be like the car commercial that proclaims, "You do so much for me!" So the false prophets have fashioned *feel-good doctrines* to accommodate our selfish desires.

Sadly, the current teachings on self-image and self-esteem, positive-possibility thinking, success and prosperity, health and wealth, each with large followings in the evangelical and charismatic world, are doomed to become some of this century's most deadly and damning heresies if those ministries and their leaders—prophets and teachers—let sinners remain comfortable and allow them to go to hell feeling good about themselves.

We do have a lot of needy and hurting people, of course, and a church must minister and counsel with a loving attitude to help and uplift those people. We are not calling for harshness. But Christ did not die for our needs, nor our hurts; He died for our sins—*and sin is supposed to be His Church's main concern.* By omitting teachings against sin, we create heresy. In a biblical ministry, an essential part of caring and healing is warning. And we must ask ourselves the question: *If sin is never mentioned and warnings never given, is the true Gospel of Christ even being preached?* If it is not, then is it not "another gospel"[21] that is being preached, and thus under the censure of the Scriptures? The apostle who turned Asia upside down and conquered it for Christ said, " But we preach Christ crucified, to the Jews a stumbling block and to the Greeks foolishness,"[22] and, "For I determined not to know anything among you except Jesus Christ and Him crucified."[23]

Most grievously, the tragedy of our times is that on the one side we have our society with blood running to its knees from the killing of its unborn, a drug epidemic, pornography, homosexual perversion, child abuse, AIDS, violence—all tearing at the fabric of society—and on the other side we have a multitude of Christian ministries that are congenially focused on preaching and teaching "peace, peace" themes, never warning the saints or the sinners about the consequences of their sins.

Such ministries commit treasonable acts against the Gospel of Jesus Christ and are unfaithful to the call of God. And like the false prophets of the Scriptures, they will receive God's searing rebuke.

The question I must ask myself is, "Will I warn them?" Have I? Or have I tried to be . . . peaceful and not stir up the waters, not cause any trouble for them— and for myself? On my day of accounting before the One who loved me and gave himself for me, one of the questions He will ask me is, "Did you warn them?" And if I answer no, He will ask me, "Why did you not?"

A False Ministry Speaks Thoughts of Its Own Mind

This is the fundamental reason why the Amaziah spirit arises, why no one turns from wickedness, why there is no warning, and why smooth themes are chosen.

The false prophets think of nothing but pleasant things for themselves. They claim that these selfish thoughts are scriptural, even given to them by the Holy Spirit, and teach these delusions to the people and give them false hopes: "They speak visions from their own minds, not from the mouth of the Lord."[24] "These lying prophets . . . prophesy the delusions of their own minds."[25] Where does the Lord place the responsibility for a nation's iniquity? At the feet of the false prophets: "Because from the prophets of Jerusalem ungodliness has spread throughout the land."[26]

F. C. Cook says, "The false prophets caused the

people to trust in lies—one being that they would not go into Babylonian captivity as Hananiah proclaimed to them [Jeremiah 28:10-11] in the dramatic way he broke the yoke which Jeremiah was wearing. They preached REBELLION against the Lord. God said they would go into captivity under the Babylonians. The false prophets, like Hananiah, prophesied they would not, which was a lie. To teach they would not, was, in effect, to teach rebellion against God."

Whenever we ministers—or any Christians—teach or even imply that we will not face accountability for our sins, or intimate that we can sin with impunity, we teach rebellion against God. We can do this simply by omitting the mention of such accountability.

False prophets place their own wisdom above the wisdom of God. If the Lord says we are to warn, that should settle the matter. False ministries, however, will not warn, because the false prophets think they know what to say better than God—they are only concerned with pleasing the people, while God is only concerned with saving their souls. False ministries squander the Word of God on the latest doctrinal fads and delusions, and do not use the Word with bold authority so that it penetrates the hearts and souls of the hearers. The most current doctrinal fad always gathers a crowd to hear "the latest revelation from the Lord," and gives the illusion of success—and a false ministry will *always* sell out the Word of God for a crowd and success—and money.

What is our Lord's attitude? "'Indeed, I am against those who prophesy false dreams,' declares the Lord . . .' They tell them and lead my people astray with their reckless lies.'"[27]

The violation of the commandment, "You shall not misuse the name of the Lord your God,"[28] is much more than vulgar cursing; it is also using the name of the Lord cavalierly to affirm some utterance of ours. IF WE

SAY THE LORD IS SPEAKING, HE HAD BETTER BE!
Caution and carefulness in our proclamations of who
is speaking is one of our best safeguards against our
ministry becoming false.

One fundamental aspect of the call to ministry that
is both beautiful and terrifying is that God has called
us because He intends to use us. This means it is our
magnificent privilege to share the Word of the Lord.
This demands seeking Him, waiting upon Him for
direction,[29] and moving only in the direction He tells
us to with the words He tells us to speak. So as a
minister, I must constantly ask myself, "Am I proclaiming every aspect of the Word of God, both that
which is pleasant to our ears and flesh, and that which
is unpleasant?"

A False Ministry Faces Judgment

We have already heard Jesus say, "Watch out for
false prophets . . . . I will tell them plainly, 'I never knew
you. Away from me, you evildoers!'" To His words,
we must add the words from the Book of Revelation:
"I warn everyone who hears the words of the prophecy
of this book: If anyone adds anything to them, God will
add to him the plagues described in this book. And if
anyone takes words away from this book of prophecy,
God will take away from him his share in the tree of
life and in the holy city, which are described in this
book."[30]

Why such harsh judgment and punishment?
Because God's Word is crucial. If we get our message
wrong, those who hear us get it wrong—and perish.
God says that if we "do not warn him [a wicked man]
or speak out to dissuade him from his evil ways in
order to save his life, that wicked man will die for his
sin, and I will hold you accountable for his blood."[31]

Ministers and their ministries, and all Christians,

face the Lord's discipline—His chastening—because He loves them, as Hebrews 12:5-11 clearly affirms. To confirm the need for such discipline and chastening, we have only to read the letters to the seven churches in which the Lord penetratingly reveals the true condition of each church, good and bad. Five times He commands a church to repent.[32]

We have seen the grievous accounts of prominent ministers who fell into sin and were publicly exposed. Their exposure should be a lesson to all of us, for our Lord's holy searchlight is on each of us in the Church— and He is looking deep within each of us to inspect and judge what we are doing and why we are doing it.

It is before the Lord that we stand when we are disciplined. He is personally dealing with each of us, and we must not—we dare not!—complain of His chastening by dismissing it as an attack of the devil or other Christians or the media. Habakkuk could not understand how God could use the pagan Babylonians to judge the people of God. It overwhelmed him. Even so, we may not understand how God can use the media to judge us, but He has used, and may continue to use, the media to probe and expose what the Church did not. God will not permit His people to do what He will judge a world for. If He will judge the world for covetousness, He will not allow it in His Church, particularly in ministers, *even if it is taught as prosperity.* He will judge and chasten us because He loves us and wants us to increasingly partake of God's divine nature and "the peaceable fruit of righteousness."[33] *Let us seek and embrace His compassionate judging.*

I may not be able to know where others stand, whether their ministries are true or false, but I can know where *I* stand. And I must know! I do myself, and those I am called to serve, the greatest service when I am tougher on myself than on anyone else and when I allow God to search me while I lay on my face before Him.

Do I want God to call me faithful, or do I want man to call me successful? Do I want the approval of man or the approval of God? Do I have a heart that only wants His "well done" or man's "great job"? Do I do what a false prophet does: put my wisdom before God's, speak peace and not warn? Do I have an Amaziah attitude? THE BOTTOM LINE: DO I FEAR GOD, OR DO I FEAR MAN?

Truth invites examination and has no fear of it. Untruth hides and covers and rationalizes and points at others. So if any of us hide from our Lord's examination and dismiss His penetrating evaluation with a casual wave of the hand, that could be a sure sign of just which side our ministry is really on.

I can hide nothing from the Lord, so it is useless to try. He knows my motives and will weigh them in *His* scales, not in mine or in societies. Each of us, alone, must confront God's examination of the motives and integrity of our ministry. King David prayed, "I know, my God, that you test the heart and are pleased with integrity, . . ."[34] and "Create in me a clean heart, O God."[35]

I may tremble in anxiety and even fear, but I must be just as forthright as David about whether what I do for God is true or false and whether my ministerial heart is clean or marred with self-delusions and falsehoods.

O God, I want to be true and clean of heart before you!

---

[1]David Payne, *Kingdoms of the Lord,* (Eerdmans, 1981), p. 207.
[2]Published by Bridge Publishing, Inc., South Plainfield, NJ 07080.
[3]Matthew 7:15 (NKJV).
[4]1 Corinthians 12:10.
[5]Matthew 7:22-23.
[6]Matthew 7:21.
[7]Acts 20:28-31.

[8]Lamentations 2:14.

[9]*The Bible Commentary, Volumes 5 and 6,* by F. C. Cook, (Baker Book House, 1981).

[10]1 Kings 18:19.

[11]Lynn Buzzard, *Freedom and Faith,* (Westchester, IL., Crossway Books, 1982), p. 21.

[12]Amos 7:10-13.

[13]Amos 7:10.

[14]Amos 7:12-13.

[15]Matthew 7:20.

[16]Jeremiah 23:14-15b.

[17]Jeremiah 6:13-14; 8:10-11.

[18]Jeremiah 23:16-17b.

[19]Jeremiah 23:19-21b.

[20]*The Bible Commentary, Volumes 5 and 6,* by F. C. Cook, (Baker Book House, 1981).

[21]2 Corinthians 11:4.

[22]1 Corinthians 1:23 (NKJV).

[23]1 Corinthians 2:2 (NKJV).

[24]Jeremiah 23:16b.

[25]Jeremiah 23:26.

[26]Jeremiah 23:15.

[27]Jeremiah 23:31-32.

[28]Deuteronomy 5:11.

[29]Isaiah 40:31.

[30]Revelation 22:18-19.

[31]Ezekiel 3:18.

[32]Revelation 1:10-3:22.

[33]Hebrews 12:10-11 (KJV).

[34]1 Chronicles 29:17.

[35]Psalm 51:10.

8

Our Greatest Need

The more Thy glories strike my eyes,
The lower I shall lie;
Thus while I fall my joys shall rise
Immeasurably high.

D. Thomas[1]

Those who have never trembled from head to toe
will never know God's perfect love.

William D. Eisenhower[2]

An American Indian was walking with a friend in a large city. The Indian stopped suddenly and looked around. "I hear a cricket," he said.

His friend said, "That's impossible with all the noise around here."

"No, I hear a cricket," the Indian said and looked around until he found the cricket.

"That's amazing," his friend said, "but I sure don't see how you managed to hear a cricket in all this city noise."

The Indian smiled and took a handful of coins out of his pocket and tossed them along the sidewalk ahead of them. People for half a block ahead stopped and started looking for the money. The Indian turned to his friend and said, "People hear what they are listening for."

What are we listening for or looking for?

One way to learn how to recognize counterfeit money is to examine genuine money carefully. If we live in a world that is false in its values and deep in iniquity and indifferent to its condition—and kept so by matching false religion and false prophets—then we need the true and certain and proven so that we can clearly see the surrounding lies. We need men and women who discern with a different ear and eye in the midst of the profusion of distractions and distortions, to show us the true and lead us away from the false. They must be like the men of Issachar, "who understood the times and knew what Israel should do."[3] They must be men and women who have gained their discernment because they know what most do not and what most care little about—*they know God!* Our most pressing need today is for men and women who *know* God—not know *about* God, but *know* God in a true Father/child intimacy. Such Christians are the urgent need of the Church today. *We can no longer continue without them!*

Lack of intimate knowledge of God is one of the basic reasons why Israel sinned. Look at what Amos and Hosea faced—a flourishing, affluent culture filled with injustice and inhumanity, coupled to an established religion and priests and prophets. Yet the people did not know God because the priests, prophets, and leaders of Israel who were entrusted with preaching and teaching them the true Word of God did not do so. So God spoke through Hosea and bluntly told them, "There is no faithfulness, no love, no acknowledgment of God in the land. There is only cursing, lying and murder, stealing and adultery; they break all bounds, and bloodshed follows bloodshed."[4]

114

Then, speaking of the consequences of this, God said, "My people are destroyed from lack of knowledge. Because you have rejected knowledge, I also reject you as my priests; . . . The more the priests increased, the more they sinned against me; they exchanged their Glory for something disgraceful. They feed on the sins of my people and relish their wickedness. And it will be: Like people, like priests. I will punish both of them for their ways and repay them for their deeds."[5]

The false ministers and religion in Israel echoed the popular public standards, and the knowledge of God was lost. Consequently, the nation reveled in its continual sins and was judged by God for them. The voice of God that was so desperately needed to save them was silent in the land. They urgently needed to hear from God, as has often been the case down through the long history of the Church. Yet it is a strange truth that God's people have almost always tried to kill or ostracize the prophets that God sent to them to speak His Word. It is as if God's message is always stronger than what they want to hear—not the soothing message they are expecting—and by killing God's messenger they can kill the message.

One of those messengers whose ears and heart were focused on God was the eminent prophet Isaiah. Isaiah spoke primarily to Judah later than the time when Amos and Hosea prophesied to Israel in the North, but his time overlapped theirs a bit. Similarly, the successful, and mostly spiritual, fifty-two-year reign of King Uzziah of Judah overlapped the prosperous forty-one-year rule of Jeroboam II of Israel. It was Uzziah who made a serious mistake and disobeyed the Lord toward the end of his reign and became leprous.[6]

Uzziah's death was a pivotal time for the nation, one filled with both apprehension and with sorrow. The sixth chapter of Isaiah begins with the words, "In the year that King Uzziah died . . . ." It was then that God

115

called Isaiah to be a prophet. In times of spiritual crisis among His people, God always raises up men and women to speak in His name, and so in that strategic year of Uzziah's death, God raised up Isaiah. Isaiah was a well-educated member of nobility who had great eloquence and access to the royal courts, so for that reason he is sometimes called the "statesman-prophet."

Isaiah's calling by God was most unusual. God actually did *raise Isaiah up*, up to heaven so that He could reveal himself to His new prophet who would have a special place in the Church's history as a truly prophetic prophet—one who would give many prophecies of the Christ to come. Although few ministers, if any, will ever have an actual encounter with God as Isaiah did, we can all read his account of it and ask God to, at minimum, reveal himself in our hearts to the same degree that He revealed himself in the vision to Isaiah.

In his vision, Isaiah saw "the Lord seated on a throne, high and exalted, and the train of his robe filled the temple. Above him were seraphs, each with six wings: With two wings they covered their faces, with two they covered their feet, and with two they were flying."[7] Derek Prince once pointed out that the action that the seraphs took with their wings was highly significant and important to us. Out of their six wings, he said, the seraphs used four to worship God and two to serve Him. Their relationship of two-thirds of their being and effort given to worship and one-third given to service, Prince said, is what the relationship of our being and effort should be in our work for God.

Isaiah heard the seraphs calling to one another, "Holy, holy, holy is the Lord Almighty; the whole earth is full of his glory."[8] The triune "holy, holy, holy" that Isaiah heard, celebrates one of the essential attributes of God. The declaration of the seraphs exalts God far above all human thoughts and conceptions. In only one other Scripture is "holy" repeated thrice—in John's vision of heaven recorded in the fourth chapter of Revelation.[9]

In Isaiah's vision, the impact of the seraphs' voices shook the doorposts and the thresholds and the Temple filled with smoke.[10] Then Isaiah said, "My eyes have seen the King, the Lord Almighty,"[11] and in seeing the Lord, he saw himself. At the sight of God's holiness, Isaiah was gripped by an overwhelming consciousness of sin, and the only way he could express his piercing awareness of his own evil was to agonizingly cry, "Woe to me! . . . I am ruined!"[12]

Isaiah saw the majestic, wondrous presence of the holy God—and in so seeing, Isaiah saw himself. The immeasurable contrast between his earthly unholiness and darkness and God's eternal holiness and glory exposed every iniquity, flaw, shortcoming, lust, false motive, wrong words, everything even remotely evil in Isaiah. Exposed were all those things that stay easily hidden in the pale light of human life.

To Isaiah, it was as if God had opened a can of worms in him and they were spilling out of his very mouth, "For I am a man of unclean lips. . . ." Then he looked around and saw everyone else, including you and me, in the same loathsome condition and continued, "And I live among a people of unclean lips."[13] Isaiah saw only one condition in those around him—corruption. He didn't see the varieties of evildoers—adulterers, fornicators, liars, murderers, abortionists, homosexuals, pornographers, the covetous, the greedy—he saw everyone with a defiled mouth, just like he saw himself.

Isaiah's woe on himself because of his evil is like David's anguish: "My bones have no soundness because of my sin. My guilt has overwhelmed me like a burden too heavy to bear. My wounds fester and are loathsome because of my sinful folly . . . . I confess my iniquity; I am troubled by my sin."[14]

About the way that God's prophets and His anointed

ones often expressed fear of Him, William Eisenhower said, "Unfortunately, many of us presume that the world is the ultimate threat and that God's function is to offset it. But the biblical position is that God is scarier than the world by far."[15]

An Earmark of a True Prophet

God's purpose for Isaiah's experience before Him was to place within Isaiah the true earmarks of caring prophets and shepherds, which are a gripping sensibility to their own sinful poverty before a holy God and a ready identification with humanity in its sin. True prophets don't stand aloof on some lofty, isolated pinnacle and hurl oaths at the derelicts below. Having had an encounter with God, they speak from a deep conviction and awareness of their own sins even as they speak to the people about their sins. From that identifying position, their words have great convicting power. True prophets, having seen God, can only say with quaking humility, "We have sinned before a holy God."

Moses had this caring essential of a prophet. When the Lord proposed to destroy Israel for its sin, Moses cried, "But now, please forgive their sin—but if not, then blot me out of the book you have written."[16] Centuries later the Apostle Paul would say, "For I could wish that I myself were cursed and cut off from Christ for the sake of my brothers, those of my own race, the people of Israel. . . . My heart's desire and prayer to God for the Israelites is that they may be saved."[17]

And see how Daniel prayed: "We have sinned and done wrong. We have been wicked and have rebelled."[18] And Nehemiah: "We have acted very wickedly toward you."[19]

A humbled heart is vital for a prophet and shepherd. Isaiah properly pronounced woe on others because of evil practices from land-grabbing to drunkenness to denial of justice to the innocents. But in a very basic sense, it does not take spiritual eyesight to inveigh against such sins in others, or against public sins; it takes only the perception of common decency. After all, women from the garden society would be expected to be against pornography or prostitution, and men from the service club would be expected to be against stealing or drugs. But their stands, though vital and commendable, are primarily motivated from customary virtue.

True prophets and shepherds, however, will not only speak against evils from the proper and expected impetus of the best interests of mankind; they will also speak from the urgency of having seen God—and in His light having seen themselves and everyone else. Thus they speak for a holy God about righteousness, about sin, about judgment, and about repentance and its blessings. True prophets and shepherds speak because they know God and because they have a sense of need and urgency. This is a crucial difference, one that every Christian and every church must know. Many may be called—or call themselves—prophets, shepherds, or pastors, but not all carry Isaiah's distinction of having seen God.

The most holy men and women of history are those who had seen God—either in a vision or deep within their hearts and souls—and thereafter walked carefully and tenderly before the Lord. They could not bear to hurt His heart and moved quickly in response to the slightest breath of the Holy Spirit, and at the first sign of God's grief over something they did, fell before Him in repentance because they did not want His displeasure for the slightest moment.

During Isaiah's vision, cleansing came by the act of one of the seraphs who took tongs and picked a live coal from the altar and flew to Isaiah and touched his mouth with it: "See, this has touched your lips; your guilt is taken away and your sin atoned for."[20] The mouth of sin was cleansed from a coal off the altar that was a foreshadow of the cross of Calvary, the earthly altar of sacrifice for the Lamb who took away the sin of the world.[21]

The word *guilt* isn't popular today. In fact, it's almost a cardinal sin for ministers to use the word because it puts people on a *guilt-trip*. Psychology has seduced us, and today we all want to appear bright and knowledgeable and psychologically in tune with the acceptable social norm. Guilt, however, is a proper word—we are guilty, very guilty, of sinning before a holy God, and we must repent or be judged and punished. Certainly there is a false guilt that can afflict tender hearts, and we must avoid that. However, this nonchalant generation doesn't have much conscience about its real and incriminating guilt. It is legitimately under judgment by a holy God, its peril is real, and it earnestly needs to face its guilt in order to save itself.

Something very significant and important to us happened when Isaiah's mouth was cleansed—his ears were opened and he heard the Lord saying, "Whom shall I send? And who will go for us?"[22] *It is a spiritually cleansed Christian who most clearly hears God.*

The clear voice of God galvanized Isaiah into action. To God's urgent question, Isaiah now had a ready answer: "Here am I. Send me!" That was what God wanted, that was what God expected, so He said to Isaiah, "Go," and gave Isaiah a message for the nation that wasn't quite what Isaiah expected.

The nation was like the Israel Amos faced— prosperous and spiritually careless, indifferent to its own sin, "ever hearing, but never understanding . . . ever seeing, but never perceiving." God left Isaiah no illusions about the task or the prospects of success from a human point of view. Isaiah's message would "make the heart of this people calloused; make their ears dull."[23] A remnant of open hearts would receive his word and be spurred to righteousness. But the greater number would tragically choose to remain in their languor, hardening their hearts to the Word of God spoken through Isaiah: "Otherwise they might see with their eyes, hear with their ears, understand with their hearts, and turn and be healed."[24]

Jesus said, "This is the verdict: Light has come into the world, but men loved darkness instead of light because their deeds were evil."[25] If people love darkness rather than light, the coming of the light brings only judgment.

Isaiah struggled with the grim prospect of continuing deadness, "For how long, O Lord?" The Lord's answer—until judgment was accomplished. But there would be a holy remnant.[26] Though God's message was not one that any prophet with a heart for the people wants to have to deliver, Isaiah had seen God in His glory—and having seen God, he would henceforth speak faithfully whatever message God gave him, regardless of the content or implications of the message.

Crucial—A Revelation of God

As it was for Isaiah, a revelation of God is vital for us, and for our world. Proverbs 29:18 says, "Where there is no revelation, the people cast off restraint; but blessed is he who keeps the law." Without a revelation, "the people cast off restraint"—they freely and openly sin; there is nothing to hold them back. Israel and Judah ignored God and committed sins without restraint.

We need restraints. But today we are casting them off in the name of freedom, even in the Church. A secularized, accommodating church without a revelation of God, without experiencing His glory in their midst, poses no threat to an idolatrous society—and we can easily see the consequences in the immoral and unspiritual conditions of most of our cities and nation.

Isaiah's vision gave him a gripping realization of his need and the need of the world. He had seen the glory of God. He had stood in awe of His wondrous holiness. He now knew God, and had a heart after Him. *He now feared God!* Because of that, Isaiah saw and heard with different ears and eyes, and he courageously spoke the Word of the Lord to his sinning nation and its distressingly indifferent people.

Where in America and the western nations are such voices? Where are the voices speaking because they *know* God, they know His holiness and speak from His heart of compassion? Where are the ministers and prophets who fear God and fear not speaking the truth of His Word? Where are the ones who will look straight into our hearts and say with a holy voice of authority, "This is the Word of the Lord, walk in it"?

We need their voices today!

Their voices are our only hope!

The Lord is again asking, "Whom shall I send, and who will go for us?"

---

[1]D. Thomas, *The Revelation of St. John the Divine*, (Pulpit Commentary, Eerdmans, 1950), p. 466.

[2]William D. Eisenhower, "Fearing God," (*Christianity Today*, February 7, 1986), p. 32.

[3]1 Chronicles 12:32.

[4]Hosea 4:1-2.

[5]Hosea 4:6-9.

[6]2 Chronicles 26:18-21.

[7]Isaiah 6:1-2.

[8]Isaiah 6:3.

[9]Revelation 4:8.

[10]Isaiah 6:4.

[11]Isaiah 6:5.

[12]Ibid.
[13]Ibid.
[14]Psalm 38:3b-5, 18.
[15]William D. Eisenhower, op. cit., p. 34.
[16]Exodus 32:32.
[17]Romans 9:3-4; 10:1.
[18]Daniel 9:5.
[19]Nehemiah 1:7.
[20]Isaiah 6:6-7.
[21]John 1:29.
[22]Isaiah 6:8.
[23]Isaiah 6:9-10a.
[24]Isaiah 6:10b.
[25]John 3:19.
[26]Isaiah 6:11-13.

9

The Cry of Compassion

This was the compassion like a God,
That when the Savior knew
The price of pardon was His blood,
His pity ne'er withdrew.

Isaac Watts

God takes into account not so much the thing we
do as the love that went to the doing of it.

Thomas à Kempis

While a pastor was sweeping his driveway, his four-year-old daughter ran past him. Just as she did, she lost her balance and fell hard to the cement, skinning her knees. As he tried to console her and stop the flow of tears, her little brother toddled over and put his tiny arms as far as he could around her and started crying, too. He wasn't physically hurt, but seeing his big sister crying made him cry. "And it was the best medicine the older girl could have," the pastor said.[1]

Jesus wept, too. And when He did, He put His arms around our world. Our world, however, has done much more than skin its knees. It has rebelled against God, willfully and continuously. We have sinned against the One who created us. So for our Lord—the One by whom, through whom, and for whom God created us[2]—to put His arms around our world was an act beyond compare. Jesus wept because He loved us.

Take a close look at our mushrooming iniquity. There is unbridled fornication in both live-in and one-night stands; there is wide acceptance of blatant homosexuality; there is debauchery in our music that is both obscene and occult; there is a drug war that is not being won; there is skyrocketing child abuse; there is daily murder in our unsafe streets; there is unrestrained violence and immorality openly shown on movie screens and television; and there is unprecedented killing of the unborn on a worldwide scale that most of us cannot comprehend. That's our modern civilization.

When we look at the sins of a nation that has the highest standard of living it has ever had, all we can do is wonder if it will ever end or if it will just get worse unless God does something about it.

Praise God! He has already done something about it. Two-thousand years ago He sent His Son to die on the cross for our sins—yours and mine.

Among places in the Scriptures where the love of God is revealed, there are particularly two with poignant examples: the prophets and the life of Christ.

The prophets spoke at crucial moments in the history of a nation or people. Through their forceful and sometimes dramatic proclamations, the prophets revealed to the people the holy God who loved them and their nation enough to confront their sins and discipline them. That was always the purpose for which God sent the prophets. No prophet was ever sent from God to say nice things about the people or nation. When the people refused to listen to the prophet, repent of their evil ways, and turn back to God, judgment came furiously as the wrath of the Lord was no longer held back from them. This happened to Israel, Judah, and most—if not all—of the nations of God's people.

We don't like to think of God being angry or wrathful, especially when we also speak of His love, because we don't see how God can be both loving and wrathful. Our lack of understanding is because we project our human responses onto God's wrath and love. His wrath is not like ours: petty, reactionary, vindictive, spiteful. Nor is His love like ours: soft, sentimental, compromising, changeable. Godet defined God's wrath as "moral indignation in all its purity . . . holy antipathy . . . without the slightest alloy of personal irritation, or selfish resentment.[3] In the same way, God's love is eternal compassion in all its purity, totally unselfish, without personal favoritism, without compromise, and as unchangeable as He is. "For I am the Lord, I do not change."[4] "Jesus Christ is the same yesterday, today, and forever."[5]

It is this love that we find so wonderfully demonstrated through the lives of His dynamic prophets and the books they wrote. The Book of Malachi, after its customary introduction, opens with God saying, "I have loved you." Jeremiah is described as "the weeping prophet." In the Book of Zephaniah, God says He "will quiet you with his love." The prophet Joel tells that God is "abounding in love." The Book of Hosea contains a portrayal of God's love that is second only to the story of Christ in His passion.

Let's look at Hosea. Hosea was a contemporary of Amos, and he gave the very last word from God to Israel just before their dreadful fall in 722 B.C. The Book of Hosea uses two human relationships to picture vividly God's love: husband and wife, and father and son. In the first relationship, God tells Hosea, "Go, take yourself a wife of harlotry and children of harlotry, for the land has committed great harlotry *by departing* from the Lord."[6]

Hosea obeys God and marries a prostitute named Gomer, and she bears him two sons and a daughter. God names each of the children and uses their names to speak to Israel.[7] Then He tells Hosea, "Go again, love a woman *who is* loved by a lover and is committing adultery, just like the love of the Lord for the children of Israel, who look to other gods and love *the* raisin cakes *of the pagans.*"[8]

By this second union, God tells Israel that though they are a whoring nation and have committed adultery against Him, the time will come when He will buy them back because He still loves them. In that day, Hosea says, "The children of Israel shall return and seek the Lord their God and David their king. They shall fear the Lord and His goodness in the latter days."[9] With God, once married is always married—because His love never changes.

The second relationship that God uses in Hosea is the imagery of a father and his son—it illustrates one of the most poignant pictures of God's compassion found anywhere in the Scriptures. I am always moved when I read the eleventh chapter of Hosea, verses one through nine. They express the caring heart of the Father toward the people of Israel who are stubbornly going their own way. Considering Israel's ungrateful rebellion, if they were our children, we would have taken a rod to them by this time. But in the Father's hand there is no rod. His hands are empty, open in compassionate grief. With Israel walking away for the very last time, the Father tries, in one final attempt, to get them to return to Him. Through Hosea, He bares His heart in grueling agony.

He begins by recounting their beautiful history together:

> When Israel was a child, I loved him, and out of
>   Egypt I called my son.
> But the more I called Israel, the further they went
>   from me.
> They sacrificed to the Baals and they burned
>   incense to images.
> It was I who taught Ephraim to walk, taking them
>   by the arms; but they did not realize it was I
>   who healed them.
> I led them with cords of human kindness, with ties
>   of love;
> I lifted the yoke from their neck and bent down to
>   feed them.[10]

Next the Father told what would happen to Israel: "Will they not return to Egypt and will not Assyria rule over them because they refuse to repent? Swords will flash in their cities, will destroy the bars of their gates and put an end to their plans."

Nevertheless, Israel was obstinate: "My people are determined to turn from me. Even if they call to the Most High, he will by no means exalt them."

Verse eight reveals the Father's broken heart. He begins with two questions: "How can I give you up, Ephraim? How can I hand you over, Israel?" Then He confesses: "My heart is changed within me; all my compassion is aroused."

Then verse nine: "I will not carry out my fierce anger, nor will I turn and devastate Ephraim. For I am God, and not man—the Holy One among you. I will not come in wrath."

Later the Father said, "I will heal their waywardness and love them freely."[11]

If we truly understand what God is saying in Hosea about His eternal relationship with His people, and thus with us, we are quiet after we read this.

We do not understand such love. And maybe we're a little uncomfortable with God's open vulnerability. Perhaps one of the most difficult things in our relationship to God is for you or me to believe that God really does love us—eternally loves us.

The Father's Greatest Cry of Compassion

To gain even greater comprehension of God's love, however, we must go to the life of Jesus—our Prophet, Priest, and King. Jesus, compelled by love, came as the Incarnate Word, stood at the crossroads of our corrupted world, and wonderfully pronounced the Father's eternal message of love, life, and righteousness. His mission for God, the Father, took Him to a cross for our sin.

Jesus was the Father's greatest cry of compassion!

In the life of Jesus, there is one particular event that brings into wonderful focus the heart of God. It is a moving moment for the Savior and a motivating one for us. It is a time when you and I look at the world through the eyes of Christ, an ennobling, transforming view; and in one sense it could be the strategic point of Jesus' ministry before Calvary.

Matthew 9:36 says, "When he saw the crowd . . . ." The crowds came and so, by today's criteria, Jesus was very successful. We love crowds. The bigger the crowds, the better. But why did the crowds come? Why did they come to hear the Son of God? For perhaps three reasons:

1. **Jesus Taught With Authority.** "The crowds were amazed at his teaching, because he taught as one who had authority, and not as their teachers of the law."[12]

Jesus had no Amaziah spirit; He was the true prophet who proclaimed what the people needed and wanted—a sure word from God. All their lives the people had *established religion* with its rituals and traditions, but they had never heard the Word of God taught with authority.

2. **Jesus Preached the Good News of the Gospel.**
He did not preach the nice news of a compromised
psychological gospel, or the dead legalisms of a sterile
religious system, or oppressive church traditions, or the
latest national or social problems, or the load of a
thousand rules—He preached good news, the Gospel of
salvation.

Where will people go to hear good news today?
Wherever they go, the news is war, drugs, abortion,
violence, moral failure, economic uncertainty, political
upheaval, social instability, and spiritual skepticism.
Where is the good news? Could they find it at church?
Or would they just find positive-possibility-faith
teachings that tell them that what the world can't get by
working, they can get by believing?

*Our Lord has placed in our hands His Word, and on our
lives His anointing, and given us an eternal spiritual message
that will lift, inspire, challenge, encourage, deliver, heal, and
convict.*

3. **Jesus Healed.** Jesus touched them. The priests,
lawyers, and Pharisees didn't do that. They didn't touch
the leper, nor the diseased, nor the sinning man or
woman. It was against their religion to do so. But Jesus
did. And with His touch, He healed every disease and
sickness, every pain and infirmity. We can't improve
on that formula for public ministry—teaching with
authority, preaching good news, healing.[13] Jesus went
everywhere doing good, healing all who were oppressed in any way.[14]

Most importantly, however, Jesus *saw* the people—
not just the crowd, but individuals: men, women,
children, babies. Let's try to stand up close and look
over His shoulder at that crowd pressing against Him
and try to sense His heart. Let's see that crowd then and
now. And let's be a bit expansive as we describe the
panorama.

131

In the crowd are all kinds of people: poor and rich, blind and deaf, demon-possessed and mentally ill, singles and married, children and old people, tax collectors and beggars, sick and well, harlots and priests, thieves and princes, the ups and the downs. They are the people at the supermarket, the gas station; the people who live on Main Street, on your street, or on my street. They are like those at my house, your house, at the Parliament House, or the White House. They are from every area on the globe—Europe, Africa, Asia, the Americas, Australia, New Zealand, and the islands of the seas. Their skin is brown, black, red, yellow, white. And there, standing not too far from Jesus, are you and me.

Jesus *sees* them. They are from diverse backgrounds: barrooms, boardrooms, brothels, sickrooms, synagogues, homes, hotels. They come from the cities, the suburbs, the country, from the military and from cloisters, from a penthouse in New York to the park in Bern. They come as they are—some holding children, some walking with canes, some in rags, some in fine clothes. They include runaway teenagers, divorcing couples, abused children, abusive parents, drunks, drug addicts, homosexuals, broken men, and degraded women.

But unlike what we too often do, Jesus *looks* at them. He doesn't see only their surfaces, He *sees* deep inside their hearts and there He sees them "harassed and helpless."[15] They are scattered sheep without spiritual direction and helpless sheep without spiritual strength. Sin produces those conditions.

In that state they have labored under the load of religion, and they are chained to religious rituals. Because of sin they are hurting, diseased, divided, and struggling. But established religion that is active but empty offers no spiritual help or hope—it doesn't confront the cardinal matter of sin It only offers rules and ceremonies and compromised theologies. Such conditions always exist in the religious community, and they certainly do today. People are responsible for the sin that brings them to this condition, but they are helpless to resolve it and are harassed by those who offer false or inadequate solutions. During His days on earth, Jesus saw them in this condition, as sheep without true shepherds to watch over them and care for their eternal souls.[16]

Some in the crowd around Jesus need only a physician or a mechanic or a dentist or a plumber to meet their needs. But there are those in the crowd who have needs that only a shepherd can meet. A parent responds to a crying infant or a lost child, and a shepherd responds to a shepherdless people. The Good Shepherd, sent from the Father, stands in the midst of this scattered, fainting crowd, and His eternal heart is pierced that they have no true shepherds to lead them. A thousand hireling shepherds have offered them insufficient remedies in return for their tithes and offerings, but the Shepherd from God sees their deep need and is moved by that alone and by His compassionate heart. As all true shepherds are, He is moved to the extent of even giving His life for the sin that He knows is the root cause of all their problems.

Deeply and powerfully, the great reservoir of love in the heart of the Lord, our Shepherd, is touched and tapped. He could have been critical. He could have berated them. He could have reminded them how they didn't follow the formula or the rules or the religious rituals they had been taught. Certainly the priests had berated them enough times about that. But Jesus was different, He had a heart of compassion that was so great that it wrapped its arms around all their faults and problems and made them His. Oh, yes, He dealt with their sins, and He warned them and called them to repentance—there was no gospel of cheap grace from Him. But first and foremost He loved them. Our Lord's eternal heart is always moved with compassion for the lost and hurting.

True shepherds and prophets with compassionate hearts are the scarcest commodities in the Church today—so scarce that when a truly compassionate shepherd or prophet appears, like Jesus or John the Baptist, the hurting and lost who have spiritual needs will come running to them.

But tragically, we seem unable to appreciate these men and women of God, instead—as they did with John the Baptist and Jesus—we kill them, not physically perhaps, but in many more painful ways. They stand before us and courageously proclaim the message that will bring life to us and healing to our land, and we destroy them. In Jesus' case, He was both the messenger and the message, and we couldn't find a cross fast enough for Him.

The moment in which Jesus sees the crowd and is moved with compassion is an especially pivotal moment for us. Jesus turns to the disciples and expresses the need He sees before Him: "The harvest is plentiful but the workers are few."[17] At that point the "laborers" were just one: Jesus. He was the only one who had been preaching, teaching, delivering, and healing. That had produced tremendous results—the lost and hurting people without true shepherds came running to Him.

The harvest in Jesus' time was great, and there is a need for laborers to match the harvest. So the metaphors that Jesus used to describe the plight of the people change—before it was sheep without a shepherd, now it is a harvest without laborers.

Having stated the spiritual problem, Jesus calls for prayer: "Ask the Lord of the harvest, therefore, to send out workers into his harvest field."[18] Facing the tremendous harvest, Jesus makes prayer the priority. It is almost as if the Lord is saying, "Stop everything, stop business, religious activity, ceremonies, services, seminars and sermons, and pray for laborers—laborers who will go into the harassed, helpless, shepherdless crowd to reap the harvest. My heavenly Father, the Lord of the harvest, has issued the summons, it demands our immediate attention!"

The prayer is soon answered, and the very disciples who prayed for laborers are themselves sent out into the fields of humanity to reap the harvest of souls. They are to do what Jesus did, and so He gives them the authority they need: "He called his twelve disciples to him and gave them authority to drive out evil spirits and to heal every disease and sickness. . . . As you go, preach this message: 'The kingdom of heaven is near.' Heal the sick, raise the dead, cleanse those who have leprosy, drive out demons. Freely you have received, freely give."[19] The disciples became part of the answer to their own prayer—what people pray about, God often involves them in.

Jesus did not preach a sentimental, shallow message, but a strong, caring one—tough and tender—a prophetic word needed by His world, our world, the whole world, every nation. In Matthew 11, for instance, Jesus commended the forceful prophetic ministry of the imprisoned John the Baptist. And He vigorously denounced the cities where He had performed miracles because they did not repent: "Woe to you, Korazin! Woe to you, Bethsaida!"[20] Yet later He spoke gently to all anxious, stressed people: "Come to me, all you who are weary and burdened, and I will give you rest."[21]

The twenty-third chapter of Matthew tells of how Jesus berated the teachers of the Law. Seven times He said, "Woe to you," and finished them off with a jolting censure: "You snakes! You brood of vipers! How will you escape being condemned to hell?"[22] Then He pronounced judgment on Jerusalem: "You who kill the prophets and stone those sent to you, how often I have longed to gather your children together, as a hen gathers her chicks under her wings, but you were not willing. Look, your house is left to you desolate."[23]

Jesus preached a direct message about repentance and judgment. He never hid the words in fancy stories or figures of speech, nor was He afraid of hurting anyone's feelings or putting a *guilt-trip* on them. He wanted all people everywhere to understand clearly what would happen to them if they did not turn back to God: "Unless you repent, you too will all perish."[24] Then in His last days, having found no prayers of repentance in the Temple, only business as usual, He wept over the city of Jerusalem and pronounced its coming judgment.[25]

For over three years, first John the Baptist and then Jesus had called the nation of Israel to repentance.[26] Solomon's Temple was the center of Israel's religious life, all national transactions with God were performed there. If the nation was going to repent, there would be a massive prayer gathering of priests, lawyers, scribes, and the people, on their faces before God, calling out their sins to Him in repentance—and the Temple would be filled with the sound and smoke of thousands of sacrifices. Instead, the business of making money was going on without interruption. When Jesus saw this on the day of His "triumphal entry" into the city,[27] He made a whip of cords and drove the merchants and money-changers out of the Temple, angrily proclaiming, "It is written, *'My house shall be called a house of prayer,'* but you have made it a *'den of thieves.'*"[28]

Jesus was a godly mixture of anger over religious indifference and compassion for the sick and hurting. He could not tolerate the self-righteous who saw no sins in themselves, but He was willing to die for the lost and repentant. Among the people struggling with the death of Lazarus, He wept with compassion and was deeply moved.[29] And just before His ascension, with His crucifixion nearing, He said, "Now my heart is troubled, and what shall I say? 'Father, save me from this hour'? No, it was for this very reason I came to this hour. Father, glorify your name!"[30]

During His torturous struggle, carrying His cross to Calvary, women followed Him mourning and wailing. Jesus said straightly to them, and to us, "Do not weep for me; weep for yourselves and for your children."[31] After He ascended to His Father, things were only going to get worse: "For if men do these things when the tree is green, what will happen when it is dry?"[32]

Jesus' message and ministry were caring and clear and complete. He left nothing out. In fact, most of what we know about hell is what Jesus told us. But how often do we think of Jesus stirred with compassion, viewing the crowd, or breathing heavily after whipping people from the Temple, or rolling in His own sweat and blood in Gethsemane, or profusely bleeding on the cross?

Can we imagine this Jesus headlining some success or self-interest Christian seminar today? Have we committed the ultimate idolatry and made Jesus into what we want Him to be—suave, urbane, congenial, prosperous, an ancient actor in a bloodless pageant that draws crowds to our Easter morning service? Have we replaced His cry and actions of compassion, His pain and suffering, with our cultured sounds and eloquent gestures?

What Kind of Jesus Do You Serve?

I remember that question being put powerfully to me and to about 125 other students in the second Bible school I attended. I was older, an upper-classman in a freshman-level class. The professor, a retired missionary in his seventies, was ramrod-straight, white-haired, and very kind; but he had eyes that seemed to look right into you.

He gave us a few days to settle into our classes, and then at the beginning of one of his classes he stood in front of us and asked, "What kind of Jesus do you serve?" He said it in a way that riveted the attention of every one of us. "Do you serve the popular Jesus now being preached, who really doesn't care how you live or what you do? Do you serve the popular Jesus who lets you go to church, kneel in prayer, then go out and be involved in questionable moral activities and go to any amusement you wish and it's all right with Him?" He continued on this way for what seemed like forever to our breaking hearts. He thrust at us penetrating question after penetrating question, each prefaced with: "What kind of a Jesus do you serve? Do you serve the popular Jesus who . . . ?"

Then he stopped, perhaps for ten seconds, looked slowly around the room, and began to weep as he quietly asked in a different voice that riveted our attention, "Or do you serve the Jesus of the Scriptures, the One who loved you so much He went to the cross?" Then he described Jesus of Nazareth, His love, His work of redemption, all in magnificent detail, and continued, "Do you serve this Jesus who loves you so much that He demands everything from you? This Jesus who wants you holy and clean and pure to be a beautiful vessel for Him, who has called you into His wonderful service . . . ." That was as far as he or we got in that class. We spent the remainder of our time that day weeping, repenting, praying, and committing ourselves to the Jesus that he knew so well, and who we wanted to know in the same way he did.

It was this Jesus, soon to return to His Father, who said, "All authority in heaven and on earth has been given to me. Therefore go and make disciples of all nations, baptizing them in the name of the Father and of the Son and of the Holy Spirit, and teaching them to obey everything I have commanded you. And surely I am with you always, to the very end of the age."[33]

This commission, and their motivating love for Christ, has sent men and women into every continent and nation in the world. They have lifted up His Name, taught in His authority, preached His good news, set people free and healed the sick. They have been true to the message—they have warned, called for repentance and holiness, exhorted for righteousness and justice—and have seen lives transformed and societies that were previously headed for judgment stirred into spiritual awakening.

Each one of these has been a special vessel, each one giving voice to the CRY OF COMPASSION that calls forth from the triune heart of the Father, the Son, and the Holy Spirit.

Let us pray for a multitude more of men and women who have a matching cry, and who will go into the highways and hedges[34] of every nation, city, town, and village to tell the people about the compassionate love of God in Jesus Christ, our Lord. Men and women like this will put their arms around our world and cry over our sins and speak to us the living Word of God that will save us.

Every nation of the world needs them NOW!

---

[1]J. David Branon, *Our Daily Bread*, (Radio Bible Class, August 1989).

[2]Colossians 1:16 (NKJV).

[3]*Godet's Biblical Studies,* Edited by W. H. Lyttleton, (London, 1985), p. 152.

[4]Malachi 3:6 (NKJV).

[5]Hebrews 13:8 (NKJV).

[6]Hosea 1:2 (NKJV).

[7]Hosea 1:3-2:23.

[8]Hosea 3:1 (NKJV).

[9]Hosea 3:5 (NKJV).
[10]Hosea 11:1-4.
[11]Hosea 14:4a.
[12]Matthew 7:28.
[13]Matthew 4:23.
[14]Acts 10:38.
[15]Matthew 9:36.
[16]John 10:7-14.
[17]Matthew 9:37.
[18]Matthew 9:38.
[19]Matthew 10:1-8.
[20]Matthew 11:21.
[21]Matthew 11:28.
[22]Matthew 23:33.
[23]Matthew 23:37-38.
[24]Luke 13:3.
[25]Luke 19:41-44.
[26]Matthew 3:1; 4:17.
[27]Matthew 21:1-11.
[28]Matthew 21:13 (NKJV).
[29]John 11:13-16.
[30]John 12:27-28.
[31]Luke 23:28.
[32]Luke 23:31.
[33]Matthew 28:18-20a.
[34]Luke 14:23 (KJV).

10

Cry for Revival

Oh, how I fear thee, living God,
With deepest, tenderest fears,
And worship thee with humble hope,
And penitential tears!

S. Conway[1]

I once heard a fable about a "First Chicken Church."
It was primarily attended by chickens from the more
fashionable part of the barnyard. It was evangelical in
its doctrines—sometimes charismatic—and there was a
strong emphasis on "chickens becoming real chickens."
This doctrine was taught at almost every meeting, and
the chickens were constantly exhorted "to use your
wings and soar." The chickens flocked to the church,
and to the seminars on good wing-waving, which
taught them how to flap with authority. And as
flapping chickens are wont to do, they bought many
books and tapes.

One particular Sunday morning, the head rooster
was especially eloquent. He crowed, "Your wings are
for flying! Use them, and rise above everything you
face." He strutted back and forth across the elegant

platform, flapped his wings enthusiastically, and demonstrated the action he expected from his congregation of chickens. Periodically throughout his sermon, and especially at the end, the church building fluttered with clapping, flapping wings. Then another great and glorious service was finished, the benediction was given, and all the flapping chickens folded their wings—and *walked* home.

We all know the pitfall of being hearers and not doers, that contradictory gulf that can exist between our proclamation and our performance. Sometimes this disparity exists because the evils of our world seem so overpowering and we find it easier and less threatening to sit in our pews and flap our wings than to actually fly. As an American Indian said after listening to a minister preach for the first time, "Much thunder, no rain."

Certainly today's challenges can appear overwhelming. The world can often appear to be chaotic, confusing, collapsing, and terminal—all at the same time. Considering its state, it may well be all of these. Some ministers try to opt out of these challenges with everything from hedonism to materialism to religious activity. But that's running from our calling just like Jonah did.

We are called to minister in this world just as it is, with all its degeneracy, and the cloud of judgment hanging over it. In fact, we're probably called to minister for the very reason that the world is in such lousy shape. Fortunately, "God has not given us a spirit of fear, but of power and of love and of a sound mind."[2]

His mandate is clear: "Go into all the world and preach the good news,"[3] and "Go and make disciples of all nations."[4] The Church is to encounter the world, to confront it, on its own territory. No place is off limits, from the farthest jungle to the nearest neighborhood, from business to education, from politics to show business, from slums to suburbs. The Commission demands our involvement, and there is no other plan.

Victory is assured. Christ said, "I will build my church, and the gates of Hades will not overcome it."[5] He has given us authority in His Name. We are to use it in prayer and proclamation. We all know this, we all profess this. But such confident talk is little more than wing-waving unless we act. Our times demand more than empty activity from the Church. Western society is swimming in blood and wallowing in immorality; it is on the brink of an eternal abyss and headed down into the depths of God's judgment. As Israel and Judah and the pagan nations fell, so we are falling. Against this backdrop, wing-waving is as pathetic as it is heretical—it would never have shaken Nineveh, and it will never shake our world.

Our day calls for resolute involvement. Our world needs the Church doing what only the Church can do—sounding forth a prophetic voice about sin and judgment. The Church must forthrightly ask itself, "If not us, who? If not now, when?" It's time for the Church to take risks, old-time risks and new-time risks; risks that may threaten reputation, status, programs, finances, even life. It's time to confront secularism and risk whatever we have to risk to do so. Our society is reaping a damning harvest. The choice in the risk will be between remaining an echo or becoming a voice—waving wings in our church or confronting sin in our world.

The choice will be difficult, perhaps agonizing—habits and preconceptions are hard to change. The temptation will be fierce to continue to echo philosophies of secularism in our message, as this would allow us to maintain our status quo and semblance of success. But the hollow toll of an echo has the clang of human wisdom placed over God's. It is the hollow sound of "peace, peace" themes that do not warn and do not turn men and women from their wicked ways. Such an echo has never brought a spiritual awakening, turned societies upside down for Christ, or brought repentance and revival. But a true prophetic voice preaching God's message has done these things scores of times.

What are we to do?

What is every church, pastor, priest, minister, and Christian to do?

Put on Our Christian Armor

The Church must develop a warfare mentality. Each member must be armed and ready to fight. Better still, each member already armed and already fighting. In today's sinning world, combat against the forces of Satan is for every Christian from grandparents to grandchildren, with no exemptions and no draft dodgers.

In a world such as ours, it will take more than manipulating messages, compromising concessions, fancy formulas, doctrinal dissertations, frivolous fads, or slangy slogans to shake it. It will take the full power of the Holy Spirit[6] convicting of sin and of righteousness and of judgment[7] through the preaching of the uncompromised Gospel of the crucified Christ.[8] Great sin is only defeated by great preaching of the victory of the cross of Christ. Such power and preaching will only come from a Church that is vigorously engaged in spiritual warfare.

Much has been said about spiritual warfare today until it has become just another formula. Usually the focus is on prayer, and that is a vital essential that we will discuss later. The Scriptures, however, concentrate more on the warriors than on the warfare, on their spiritual preparedness, on their spiritual character. They must have on their spiritual armor. In the sixth chapter of Ephesians, verses ten through twenty tell us to stand in the day of evil and lists the "whole armor of God" that Christians are to put on so that we *can* stand: the belt of truth, the breastplate of righteousness, the shoes of readiness, the shield of faith, the helmet of salvation, and the sword of the Spirit which is the Word of God. Each part of God's armor comes from the character of Christ—indeed, is Christ—and each is suited to protect us today. For instance, there is the belt of truth in a day of clever lies that rationalize enormous sin, and the breastplate of righteousness in a day of foul evil—personal holiness as protection is vital. Any Christian who fights without armor is not ready and is certain to become a casualty.

For an armored Christian there are two elements to spiritual warfare: bold intercessory prayer, and bold biblical preaching. Both—together, not separate—will bring down the powers of darkness wherever they are found. The rise of intercessory prayer today is most heartening. I pray it will continue. But intercessory prayer must now be accompanied by strong, scriptural preaching that will leave nothing out, preaching that will include warnings of the consequences of sin and the resulting judgment.

Furthermore, our prayer and preaching must be motivated by the heart of God—they must be cries of compassion both in the secret place seeking God on behalf of the land, and in the public place proclaiming God's Word to the land. We will also discuss these presently.

Again, however, it is the holy character of the warrior that is fundamental to readiness. Basic to developing that holy character is repentance. Repentance develops that humble, sturdy character that relies on the Lord, stands strong in His power, and lives a holy life.

The Priority of Repentance

Repentance includes seeking and embracing the Lord's discipline. Before the Church can speak with conviction about sin, she must be convicted about her own—before she can preach about judgment, she must be judged herself. Our Lord will not permit in His Church those things for which He will judge a world: "For it is time for judgment to begin with the family of God."[9] In chapters two and three of the Book of Revelation, we can see how Christ personally and strongly evaluated His Church in His letters to the seven churches. When God began to deal with the sin of Judah, shown to Ezekiel in a vision, He commanded, "'Begin at my sanctuary.' So they began with the elders who were in front of the temple."[10] God not only began in the house of God, He began with the elders in the house of God—elders who were worldly, cold of soul, compromised. Judgment begins at the house of God, and *it begins with the older Christians who are in the house of God.* Let this be a warning to every Christian named an elder, and to those who have been Christians long enough so that they should be mature in their walk with the Lord.[11]

For any Christian or church to be truly effective today and stand ramrod-straight while giving God's prophetic messages to our sinning, idolatrous, and violent world, they must be openly under the Lord's loving discipline. We must aspire to be an open book, transparent before the Lord and all who examine us. We face the intense scrutiny of the world, a scrutiny that will only get more fierce with the passing of time. That scrutiny quickly picks up our phony pious facades, and we delude ourselves grandly when we think we really fool anyone—the world, Christians, God, Christ, or the Holy Spirit. The only ones we fool are ourselves.

To be genuine today, and readied for warfare, there are two sins Christians particularly need to bare and repent of—idolatry and murder. It is easy to speak of these sins as being "in the world" and not admit to their being "in the Church," where they also exist.

Our secular society is idolatrous. The vacuum created from living as if God were not there is filled by idolatry, and our idolatrous mindset easily rationalizes our devastating sins. One definition of idolatry is "assigning ultimate value to things that are only temporal." What we love shows where our heart is and what we treasure. Idolatry can be either idols or ideals.

God is love, and He is the One who has ultimate value. God also loves, but He only loves what has ultimate value. He does not love the temporal, that which will one day pass away. In this world, the only creatures who have ultimate value—and ultimate destiny—are those God created in His own image: human beings—you and me, everyone. Jesus put things in perspective when He spoke of the birds that the Father cares for, and then said, "Are you not much more valuable than they?"[12] Jesus then tells us something that should draw our focus away from idolatrous concern about what we have to wear or eat or drink: "For the pagans run after all these things, and your heavenly Father knows that you need them."[13]

You or I—who have ultimate value and destiny—are idolatrous to the degree that we invest ourselves (our time, energy, and money) primarily toward things that are temporal. So where *is* our focus? On God? On those who are made in His image and have ultimate value to Him, those whom He loves and who are in sin and lost? Or is our focus on this world and our desire for things in it? How much of our focus is dominated by transient concerns? In our churches, how much time and money is spent on providing creature comforts? Do we define Christian success in materialistic terms, in how much we own, what kind of car we're driving, how big our house is, how many people attend our church? Have we Christianized greed with our gain-is-godliness[14] philosophy? Is all this idolatry?

Right here we need to get tough on ourselves, very tough. If we intend to have credibility when we confront our idolatrous world with sin and judgment, we need to spare nothing and deal severely with our own idolatry. One thing the idolatrous can spot is another idolater, especially a Christian idolater.

The other sin we need to uncover and repent of is the spirit of murder in the Church. Murder might be defined as "the action of one or more humans to either destroy or degrade another human being." The heinous foulness of the sin of murder is its essential assault on the unrepeatable miracles God made in His own image. The attack can be outright killing, or it can be debasement. This means that degrading sins such as gossip, slander, backbiting, hatred, anger, and abuse are all part of the sin of murder. Jesus said that anyone who was angry with someone or called them a fool was in danger of being judged for breaking the commandment, "You shall not murder."[15]

As a practical matter, therefore, we can trace both the sin of abortion and the sin of gossip to the same spirit of murder—what motivates the abortionist also motivates the slanderer or gossiper. There is no difference in the root impetus that wants to expel from the womb an unborn child by killing it, or wants to expel from fellowship a brother or sister in Christ by debasing them.

Local churches can be "abortuaries."[16] Look at the things that plague and destroy congregations: the censorious attitudes, the suspicions raised among church members about each other, the murmuring against pastors, the gainsaying, the backbiting, the rejection—all of it assaulting those God loves and for whom Christ died. In our disunion, we shift from church to church so that instead of building the Kingdom we continually rearrange it. Thereby one church and pastor's grief over division becomes another church and pastor's revival. We have so seared our consciences to the brutality of the spirit of murder in the Church that we destroy one another just as easily as the nation performs abortions, and we do it with abandon and without conscience or remorse. This is the defining sin of the Church. In addition, we often add the sin of hypocrisy to our crime by being smugly and superiorly "spiritual" while we wield the knife. There is no difference in God's eyes between physical murder and psychological and spiritual murder. To Him one is not worse than the other.

Perhaps the largest and most important question we can ask ourselves is, *How can a Christian or a church confront a violent world that has blood up to its waist when the Church has blood up to its heart?* It can't! That's one of the main reasons why the Church is ineffective today in confronting abortion—the Church has done little to confront the bloodshed in its own midst. It does not call the slaughter within its walls "sin," it tolerates it as the way church life is. If adultery and gossip are both committed in the Church—and both are equal sins in the sight of God—who is the more likely to be censored, the adulterer or the gossiper?

Revival will come when gossip is as grievous to the heart of a Christian as abortion is. In fact, as the history of revivals shows, grief over hurting your brother or sister in the family of God will probably be one of the keys that opens the door to revival. The Moravian Revival of 1727 resulted in a prayer meeting that ran continuously for over 100 years and in missionaries being sent all over the world. Read what John Boehme says about the way the revival began:

On August 13, 1727, as 300 believers gathered together for prayer, the Holy Spirit brought deep conviction of sin on the group. The whole community was engulfed in the stark realization of their wretchedness before God and their need of repentance. One by one, they confessed and forsook the grievances which had grown up between them over the years. Tears and forgiveness flowed freely, and the Moravian revival had begun.[17]

In this light, look again at Isaiah's agonizing lament: "Woe to me! . . . I am ruined! For I am a man of unclean lips, and I live among a people of unclean lips."[18] Isaiah could include among the foul excrement he saw coming through his lips not only that of the foul language in dirty stories, but of filth spewed on others in slander and gossip and murmuring.

May we repent of the spirit of murder. May the repentance come as we view one another through the eyes of Christ. Then we will have the moral fortitude to confront a murderous society and command it to repent.

Another sin that each Christian and church must face is *spiritual apathy*. Materialism, worldliness, distractions, fads, and mere religious activity all lead to spiritual apathy and will leave our world without a witness. We will betray our God-given position as watchmen[19] because we have fallen into spiritual slumber and are no longer interested in watching out for the souls of lost men, women, and children.

Ernie Abella, a humble, gentle-spirited man from the Philippines, spoke in a summer camp in the United States in 1990. He said, "The Church is to be prophetic in the sense that it needs to be speaking the mind of God in particular circumstances. It is not just meant to foretell an event that will be coming. The prophetic church will be a forth-telling voice. That is, it will be speaking what God thinks of a particular situation."

Those who heard him said he then spoke prophetically and forcefully:

> Your nation will be shaken so that there will be passion in your prayers. The reason there is no passion in your prayers is because your hearts have become fat. You are dying from obesity of the spirit. You are not giving out as you ought to be . . . .You will die in your fatness. You will look up and say, "O Lord, what is happening?" There will be no answer because in the day of your visitation, you did not respond to the calling of God . . . . Some of you ask, "What does God want us to do?" God is saying to you, "You have stopped listening to me because you have chosen to stay in your comfortable churches. You are meant to be light to the nations. But how will the nations hear and see unless you go? . . . You are to cry, you are to repent, you are to seek the forgiveness of your God because you have had so much, received so much and yet you do not act on what you have heard.[20]

The impact was so profound many fell on their knees, others fell on their faces, and all over the building Christians began to weep and cry out to the Lord. There was repentance and travail. Deep intercession continued for over an hour.[21]

If we want something like this to happen, we must desire it, and we must aspire to be dealt with about it by the Lord. One healthy spot to start studying repentance is to open the Scriptures to the Book of Revelation, chapters two and three, and allow our Lord to examine us from the letters to the seven churches. His probing will be balanced, fair and loving, as He has the best in mind for us and for His Church. We may tremble when He says, "I know your deeds," but He will commend what is good and rebuke only what is not.

Five times in the letters, Christ says, "Repent," and we should let this word impact us and penetrate us. Ask the Holy Spirit, "Am I like Ephesus, having high standards, persevering, active, hard-working, but having lost my first love?" If so, repent! "Am I like

Pergamum, remaining true to His name, but tolerating the immoral teaching of Balaam as well as the teaching of the Nicolaitans?" Repent! "Am I like Thyatira, having love and faith and perseverance, but compromised by Jezebel?" Repent! "Am I like Sardis, having a reputation of being alive, but am dead, and needing to wake up?" Repent! "Am I like Laodicea, neither cold nor hot, but lukewarm, about to be spit out by the Lord; thinking I am fine, but really poor, wretched, pitiful, blind?" Repent! Philadelphia has only commendation. So does Smyrna. Why? Examining those two letters will tell us. For the sake of our relationship to the Lord and our work for Him, let's dig deeply into each of the seven letters, and allow the Holy Spirit to test our motives and speak to us.

Every pastor should prostrate himself regularly before the Lord with these seven letters and ask which of the seven churches his church most closely resembles. Let the elders do it as well. It will probably be a shaking, but cleansing, moment of truth, for nothing escapes the Holy Spirit's view. Pretenses, facades, false emphasis, wrong programs, idolatry, and the spirit of murder will be exposed and reproved by Him—and their opposites will be shown and commended.

We should also examine ourselves before the Beatitudes in the Gospel of Matthew, chapter five, verses one through twelve. Start with questions: "Am I poor in spirit, admitting my spiritual bankruptcy before God? Do I mourn over the things God mourns over, such as sin? Am I meek, abandoned to the will of God? Do I hunger and thirst for righteousness—do I really want to know Him above all else? Am I merciful, showing grace and care to others? Am I pure in heart, clean, transparent, open? Am I a peacemaker, one who binds, brings together in love? When I am persecuted, do I rejoice?"

Each of these questions has an answer containing a

powerful promise. Study them. Growing in the graces of the Beatitudes moves us toward being savory salt and the bright lights of our world that Jesus spoke of in verses thirteen and fourteen. Developing in the Beatitudes will bring confrontation with our sins. As salt and light we will stand the world's scrutiny, and reveal their lack of flavor and their darkness.

The Cry of Intercession

Intercessory prayer is one of the crucial elements of spiritual warfare. Christians, churches, pastors, priests, and ministers must urgently place intercessory prayer at the center of their agenda! Intercessory prayer is not to be a peripheral part of the Church, it is to be central. It is not to be a ministry, it is to be *the* ministry. Intercession is the Church again doing what only the Church can do. Intercession becomes urgent when the warnings of the Scriptures are taken seriously. The intercessors, however, do not fatalistically step aside and allow "the inevitable" to happen because a sinning society is headed for judgment. The intercessors go to their knees and plead the sinners' case before God. Such intercessory prayer is love on its knees raising a cry of compassion to the Father.

Now let's return to the prophet Amos. We have examined how he spoke God's Word to a nation that continued sinning right on into judgment. However, chapter seven of the Book of Amos begins five visions that Amos had that have a different ending. In the first vision, the prophet was shown a swarm of locusts coming to the land just *after* the king's share had been harvested and just *before* the second crop which went to the people. When Amos saw the locusts strip the land, he cried out, "Sovereign Lord, forgive! How can Jacob survive? He is so small!" The Lord heard Amos's prayer and relented.[22]

In the second vision, Amos saw judgment by fire which "dried up the great deep and devoured the land." Again Amos cried out: "Sovereign Lord, I beg you, stop! How can Jacob survive? He is so small!" Once more the Lord heard Amos's prayer and relented.[23]

In both visions, Amos interceded in prayer. The coming devastation so gripped him that he cried out on Israel's behalf. Did Israel deserve judgment? Yes. Did the Lord respond to intercession? Yes.

We should also look at Ezekiel 22 when Jerusalem was headed for judgment because of their sin. In the first twenty-nine verses of the chapter, the iniquity of the city is described. Eight times the Lord said the city had shed blood. Once Ezekiel was asked, "Will you judge this city of bloodshed?"[24] Twice Ezekiel heard the indictment: "O city that brings on herself doom by shedding blood . . . you have become guilty because of the blood you have shed."[25] Ezekiel named the officials who were ". . . like wolves tearing their prey; they shed blood and kill people to make unjust gain."[26] In addition, Jerusalem had that tragic problem: false prophets who "whitewashed" these deeds for them by false visions and lying divinations.[27]

The city was dying in its sins. But what did the Lord want? "I looked for a man among them who would build up the wall and stand before me in the gap on behalf of the land so I would not have to destroy it, but I found none."[28] The Lord did not want to judge; no, He was looking for someone to stand before Him on behalf of the land so that judgment would not come. It is true that we need to take our stand before the world, but our first place is to stand before the Lord in intercession.

Our intercession should be repentance on behalf of the country—in the first person plural: "We have sinned." Read the prayers of such men as Daniel (chapter 9), Ezra (chapters nine and ten) and Nehemiah (chapter one) who prayed this way. Repentance must be led in the community by Christians repenting first. Let the world see our repentance.

Joel called for such repentant prayer. The nation had sinned, and the land had been devastated: "The fields are ruined, the ground is dried up; the grain is destroyed, the new wine is dried up, the oil fails."[29] There was a spirit of depression: "Surely the joy of mankind is withered away."[30] The times were terminal: "Alas for that day! For the day of the Lord is near; it will come like destruction from the Almighty."[31]

The top priority was for the nation to repent. So Joel called for priests to lead the prayers of repentance. For this purpose they were to call a solemn assembly, blow the trumpet, call for fasting, and gather everyone from the elders to the children, even nursing babies. Prayers were to take priority over every activity, even weddings.[32]

The Lord wanted them to return to Him wholeheartedly with no reservations, completely turning themselves over to the Lord. "Return to me with all your heart." That wholeheartedness included fasting, weeping, and mourning.[33]

They were to return to Him brokenhearted: "Rend your heart and not your garments."[34] The tearing of the garments was an ancient way of outwardly showing grief, but it could also be merely an outward action without a corresponding inward grief of the heart. It could be an empty ritual. The Lord calls for us to come to Him with a heart truly broken over sin. Coming to the Lord wholeheartedly and brokenheartedly is difficult, but it is possible because the Lord is tenderhearted: "For he is gracious and compassionate, slow to anger and abounding in love, and he relents from sending calamity."[35]

Today the Church should set the priority to seek the Lord in this way "on behalf of the land." Only after we repent of our own sins will we be able to lead the country in repenting of its sins.

In our intercession there should be spiritual warfare, binding the powers of darkness and releasing the power and anointing of the Lord. There should be prayer against the spirit of murder, immorality, and idolatry. There should be prayer for a mighty revival in the Church and for spiritual awakening in the community.

May the agenda of intercessory prayer come to every church and be led by the pastors, priests, and ministers. In our own ministry, we have employed intercessory prayer in three ways. One was a "seventy-two-hour prayer meeting." We would go around the clock in the church prayer room in one-hour and two-hour segments from 9:00 P.M. Sunday to 9:00 P.M. Wednesday. We started at about the end of the Sunday night service and ended with the final two hours of the midweek service when testimonies from participants would be shared.

There would be several such prayer meetings a year, announced weeks in advance. A large sign-up poster was put in the vestibule. The hours from midnight to 6:00 A.M. were three two-hour segments restricted to couples or men. We did allow people to pray at home, but we made every effort to have at least one person in the prayer room every hour. We encouraged people to fast as personally directed by the Holy Spirit. People handed in prayer requests, and I prepared a suggested Scripture and schedule for an hour of prayer.

Another arrangement was a day of fasting and prayer going from sundown Saturday to sundown Sunday. These were priority times, announced usually a couple of months ahead so that family schedules could be coordinated. On that Sunday, we would meet for early prayer, then hold our regular morning service. After the benediction, we would immediately gather with those staying to pray, and we would seek the Lord together until around 1:30 P.M.

These Sunday times were motivated by Ezekiel 22:30 (NKJV), where it is recorded that the LORD said, "So I sought for a man among them who would make a wall, and stand in the gap before Me on behalf of the land, that I should not destroy it; but I found no one." In the prayer meeting, we would repent of personal sins and public sins and cry out to the Lord for revival. In the newspapers and on television, we would announce the time of repentance for sins such as abortion, pornography, idolatry, racism, humanism, and all other sins for which we were going to intercede. We invited other churches to join in. A third arrangement was daily early morning prayer. Men and women would come into the prayer room at various times from 4:00 A.M. to 7:00 A.M.

These were times when we saw many answers to prayers. These were also special times of bonding in fellowship as Christians labored together in this important way. In that community, prayer became the joint activity among many of the churches. In November, 1986, there was an eight-day, around-the-clock, inter-church prayer meeting from Sunday to Sunday inclusive.

The great evangelist, Charles Finney, knew he was only as strong as his ability to pray: "Unless I had the spirit of prayer, I could not do anything. If I lost the spirit of grace and supplication even for a day or an hour, I found myself unable to preach with power and efficiency or to win a soul by personal conversion."

So let the Church put on God's armor and become a people who cry out to God over sins—a repenting and interceding people. A crying people are motivated by three realities: one, the grievous sin of the culture; two, the compassion of the Lord, who is ready to forgive when we repent; three, the coming judgment for unrepented sins.

There are three keys to doing all this: the *will* to do it, the *will* to begin, the *will* to begin NOW.

The goal is revival.

The trophy is eternal souls for God.

[1]S. Conway, *The Revelation of St. John the Divine, Pulpit Commentary*, (Eerdmans, 1950), p. 31.

[2]2 Timothy 1:7 (NKJV).

[3]Mark 16:15.

[4]Matthew 28:19.

[5]Matthew 16:18.

[6]Luke 4:14.

[7]John 16:8-11.

[8]1 Corinthians 1:23; 2:2.

[9]1 Peter 4:17.

[10]Ezekiel 9:6.

[11]Hebrews 5:12-14; 6:1-2.

[12]Matthew 6:26.

[13]Matthew 6:32.

[14]1 Timothy 6:5.

[15]Matthew 5:21-22 (NKJV).

[16]A coined word.

[17]John Boehme, "The Moravians, A Model of Revival for Our Times."

[18]Isaiah 6:5.

[19]Ezekiel 3:17; 33:2-7.

[20]Ernie Abella, quoted in *World Map Digest*, 1990, pp. 12-13.

[21]Ibid., p. 13.

[22]Amos 7:1-3.

[23]Amos 7:4-6.

[24]Ezekiel 22:1.

[25]Ezekiel 22:3-4.

[26]Ezekiel 22:27.

[27]Ezekiel 22:28.

[28]Ezekiel 22:30.

[29]Joel 1:10.

[30]Joel 1:12.

[31]Joel 1:15.

[32]Joel 2:15-16.

[33]Joel 2:12.

[34]Joel 2:13.

[35]Ibid.

11

Precise About Sin

> It is demanded of Christians: "Is this sin?" Their testimony must be given on this subject. They are God's witnesses . . . . Consequently, the silence of Christians upon the subject is virtually saying that they do not consider slavery as a sin. The truth is, this is a subject on which they cannot be silent without guilt.
>
> *Charles G. Finney*

Three things seem to be avoided in churches: front seats, third verses of four-verse hymns, and the mention of sin. That's a cardinal difference between God and man: God makes much of sin, man makes little of it—and today, so does the Church.

In the days of the great revivals, however, the revival preachers were determined to be accurate about sin. Jesus hadn't yet come upon the scene when John the Baptist was preaching, "Repent, for the kingdom of heaven is near." John the Baptist seared the Pharisees and Sadducees with his words: "You brood of vipers! Who warned you to flee from the coming wrath? Produce fruit in keeping with repentance."[1] The fruit of his powerful preaching was that people were continually coming to him and "confessing their sins." Of this kind of preaching, the colorful Billy Sunday once said to a large audience, "If this rubs the fur the wrong way, turn the cat around."

Many see such preaching as harsh, unloving, but true compassion is precise about sin.

"Sin" is a jolting, convicting word that most sinners don't like, so to accommodate them we have made an art form of finding euphemisms to soften the impact. Today we have problems, hang-ups, needs, sometimes evils, even demons, but not much sin. Phrases and words like "premarital sex," "extramarital affair," and "promiscuousness" have so subtly infiltrated our language that we never noticed that polite society was using them to replace *fornication, adultery,* and *whore-mongering*. We kill our unborn children and call it "terminating pregnancy," and outside the womb the aborted child is no longer a dead baby, but "a collection of tissue." Christians aren't exempted from changing words to make their sins respectable; for example, today in the Church we don't gossip, we "share."

There is a pressure today to tone down sin, to move toward permissiveness. It's an insidious process that the Church should not tolerate. As Professor Blairlock said, in this process, that which once stirred shame and revulsion is first tolerated, then accepted, and finally embraced. Dr. John Court recalled that years ago psychology textbooks described homosexuality as sexual "perversion"; later it became sexual "deviance," then sexual "orientation," and today it is sexual "preference."[2]

That word "preference" is big today. It means right or wrong being defined by the preferences of society at any given moment. For instance, sin is not in killing our unborn, sin is not giving the unlimited right to do so. Or sin is destroying a spotted owl's habitat, not in killing our unborn. Sin today is whatever society decides is socially, politically, or environmentally incorrect. Mary Stocks observed: "We don't call it sin today, we call it self-expression."[3]

But misnaming something that is deadly is perilous. My wife, Esther, tells about a time on her family's ranch, high and isolated in the Colorado Rockies, when two of her brothers, Jesse and John (aged about nine and eleven at the time), went fishing several miles from the house. The two got caught up in their activity and didn't start home until it was getting dark. En route they heard what they thought was the family cat. They called out, "Here, Kitty Tom! Here, Kitty Tom!" Instead of a cat meow, the response was the heart-stopping scream of a mountain lion a few yards away. Terrified, they fled at top speed for home. Mother and father were momentarily away and an older sister was in charge. The two boys were so panicked when they dashed into the ranch house and told their story that they terrified their brothers and sister, and all of them scurried up into the attic and laid a bed over the trapdoor.

Over the years, Esther's family has laughed over that episode. Those boys were certainly in danger when they encountered the mountain lion, although probably not as much as their frightened imaginations made them believe. But they certainly were not near the peril we are in today when we face deadly sins and purposely rename them so we won't feel any convicting guilt. When the two boys realized their mistake, they ran. We don't run because we're not alarmed—we've made our sins socially and politically correct.

But from eternity past to eternity future, God hates sin. There has never been, nor will there ever be, a diminishing in any degree of God's absolute hatred of sin. There has never been, nor will there ever be, a diminishing in any degree of God's absolute hatred of unmarried couples living together, of premarital or extramarital sex; or of cursing, gossiping, greed, or killing innocent life.

A Christian catch-phrase is, "We are to hate the sin, and love the sinner." True enough, if understood. But we do neither. God does both. We do not hate sin with the deep, eternal revulsion with which God hates it. Nor do we love the sinner with the great, compassionate heart of the Father. For us, the phrase means "tolerate the sin, and excuse the sinner." But it really doesn't matter how we phrase it or how we say it. In the Day of Judgment, there will be no distinction between sinners and their sins—sinners will stand before God to be judged for their sins, and not having repented of them on earth, they will face the eternal hatred of God and will remain under His wrath forever in the Lake of Fire.

John 3:18 says, "Whoever believes in him [Christ] is not condemned, but whoever does not believe stands condemned already because he has not believed in the name of God's one and only Son." And in Romans 1:18 it is written, "The wrath of God is being revealed from heaven against all the godlessness and wickedness of men who suppress the truth by their wickedness."

Calling a sin something that makes us comfortable numbs our consciences against evil and decreases the possibility of our ever repenting, for it is the guilt and weight of our sins that brings us to repentance. By not mentioning sin we effectively remove holiness and justice from God's character, thus we make Him no God at all, certainly not the holy God of the Bible. A not-so-holy God who doesn't mind sin is one that we have fashioned after our own image, and that means we have created an idol to worship.

Society's hedonistic selfishness has made feeling good virtually a greater right than other concerns. If marriage is making you feel bad: (a) get another spouse and trash the wedding vows; (b) take a lover and practice adultery; (c) divorce, fornicate with a live-in. But you must not feel bad. If a pregnancy will inconvenience you, kill your unborn baby—you have a right to feel happy.

The Church's message has adapted this emphasis so that when we sin, we don't think of getting right with God, but of finding some way to feel good again. We want to get rid of bad feelings, not of sin. It doesn't occur to us that the reason we feel bad is because of sin.

We've also made God a genie whose power we can use to obtain success, happiness, and earthly benefits. Personal success is our message focus, not personal salvation. The Church seeks growth through being congenial and obliging, not by being consecrated and humble.

The packaging of Christ by the Church, in this age of congenial pluralism, avoids presenting Him as the *only* option for mankind, but rather makes Him but one option of many. So we would rather say Christ is the best option, the preferred option, that He is there to meet your needs and care for your problems; but we balk at focusing on Christ as the exclusive Savior and Lord. We get uncomfortable with Christ's own narrowness: "I am the way and the truth and the life. No one comes to the Father except through me,"[4] and with Peter's and the early church's tight focus on Christ: "Salvation is found in no one else, for there is no other name under heaven given to men by which we must be saved."[5]

"Come to the Lord," we say in our invitations; but Jesus warned us that not everyone who says "Lord, Lord," will enter the Kingdom of heaven, but only those who do the will of the Father in heaven.[6] We can only "come to the Lord" with repentance of sin. R. C. Sproul said, "To embrace Jesus without repenting of sin is to be numbered among the workers of lawlessness who cry to Jesus 'Lord, Lord,' to whom Jesus will respond:

'I never knew you: depart from me, you that work iniquity.'"[7] How many people sitting in churches—evangelical, Pentecostal, charismatic, Catholic—are in the deadly spiritual situation of Christians who have said "Lord, Lord," but never repented of sin?

We believe we know better than God how to approach people, so we refrain from mentioning sin. We've persuaded ourselves that appeals to personal success, self-interest, or prosperity are better. However, just four verses into the Book of Isaiah, God had Isaiah saying to Judah, "Ah, sinful nation, a people loaded with guilt, a brood of evildoers, children given to corruption! They have forsaken the Lord."[8] Judah was a self-congratulatory nation who thought they were pretty good, then God had Isaiah tell them they were filthy sinners.

We sometimes cover our approach by stressing that our emphasis is just good pre-evangelism or public relations that avoids legalism. But such an excuse can be self-delusion, especially when we're really putting our wisdom above God's and speaking visions from our own mind.

Tragically, today's secularistic, live-for-the-now philosophies produce despair—one of today's earmarks is massive meaninglessness. After all, if this is all there is, and you and I are all there are, well, that's grim. And when we accommodate today's secular philosophy into our own message, we aid the spirit of despair. When our message centers on concerns of only now, it becomes shallow, self-centered optimism championed as truth, promising much but empty, leaving the world without real hope.

Among the things that only the Church can do—and must do—is to confront our now-centered society by speaking to ultimate issues: eternity, sin, accountability to God, grace, mercy, heaven, and hell. There is powerful optimism in the Gospel—faith-filled, joyful and eternal—but it's not shallow, because it's precise about sin.

A compassionate voice will be precise about sin, otherwise it will wallow in sentimentalism. Sentimentalism just pities the sinner and takes the sinner's side in his sin instead of God's, ignoring that the sinner is a willing rebel against God. God is love, and He loves sinners—for which we rejoice—but He is exact about evil and sin bringing death. A true compassionate voice will have the same firm and clear view of sin that God has.

Jesus Was Precise About Sin

When He was on the earth, Jesus was precise about sin: "Woe to the world because of the things that cause people to sin! . . . If your hand or your foot causes you to sin, cut it off and throw it away. It is better for you to enter life maimed or crippled than to have two hands or two feet and be thrown into eternal fire. And if your eye causes you to sin, gouge it out and throw it away. It is better for you to enter life with one eye than to have two eyes and be thrown into the fire of hell."[9]

"Woe." "Cut it off." "Gouge it out." Jesus goes after the cancer that is killing us. He doesn't just prescribe a larger dose of painkiller. If your immorality may give you AIDS, cut out the sinful behavior.

Paul was precise about sin. In the first chapter of Romans, the dark list includes "every kind of wickedness, evil, greed, depravity . . . envy, murder, strife, deceit and malice," with "gossips, slanderers, God-haters, insolent, arrogant and boastful," who "invent ways of doing evil . . . disobey their parents . . . senseless, faithless, heartless, ruthless."[10]

This list describes you and me. We have the ability to do everything on the list. Take a pen and draw a straight line down a piece of paper. On the left of the line put "Hitler." On the right of the line put "God." Using "Hitler" as a metaphor for the very worst of human beings contrasted with the perfect holiness of God, ask where on the line between Hitler and God you would put yourself. Comparing ourselves to the righteous God, honesty puts us near Hitler.

The Bible is precise about sin—and graphic! "All of us have become like one who is unclean, and all our righteous acts are like filthy rags."[11] The Bible tells us that someone who returns to sin is like a dog who returns to his vomit,[12] and it describes the throats of sinners as "open graves."[13]

But society—and many churches—are not precise about sin. The fence has been torn down and we sin with abandon. One sin practiced wantonly is killing our unborn, which is not considered sin by a large section of society. One key reason abortion is not considered sin is because of clever deceptions. Three are prevalent:

Playboyism. One of the dominant attitudes of errant manhood is the playboy mentality. This modern hedonism promotes fornication, adultery, whore-mongering, and other sexual sins. Abortion is welcomed in the playboy philosophy. The playboy doesn't want a pregnant plaything, so he's glad to have the intruding unborn killed. The playboy philosophy allows men to abandon their unborn children. Abortion is one of the cleverest oppressions with which men have deluded women.

Amos confronted the complacent, pleasure-focused notable men of Israel: "You lie on beds inlaid with ivory and lounge on your couches. You dine on choice lambs and fattened calves . . . . You drink wine by the bowlful, and use the finest lotions." He had one chilling statement to them: "Woe to you!"[14] They would be among the first to be judged.

Feminism. Most feminists are pressing for the right to kill the unborn. This is at the core of their agenda.

They work to control public opinion and pressure public officials so that killing our unborn can remain officially sanctioned. They look on woman's God-given capacity to conceive and bear children as reproductive oppression, restricting their capability to compete with men. They want women and women alone, of whatever age, to have the sole and absolute right to decide on killing the unborn.

Amos faced the women of Israel and said, "Hear this word, you cows of Bashan . . . you women who oppress the poor and crush the needy."[15] They would also be among the first to be judged

Environmentalism. Saving our environment is a worthy goal. There is nothing wrong with having clean air, conserving energy and resources, caring for our forests and wildlife, and similar efforts. But today, environmentalism is a gallery for our upside-down values: We protect eagle eggs and kill our unborn. We cry to save an animal species, but never blink at destroying our own children in the womb. Nations will arise in international friendship to save two whales trapped in Arctic ice, but easily throw their developing babies into the rubbish. Put up a picture of a cute, white baby seal bludgeoned to death for its fur, with its blood oozing onto the snow, and you get sympathy; put up a picture of an aborted unborn baby and you get scorn.

Hosea capped the summary of Israel's sins with: "bloodshed follows bloodshed."[16] Israel was sanctioning the shedding of innocent blood. Hosea followed up with: "Because of this the land mourns, and all who live in it waste away; the beasts of the field and the birds of the air and the fish of the sea are dying."[17] Israel also had environmental decay. The cause: sin. The remedy: repentance.

In the Scriptures, particularly in the writings of the prophets, the condition of the land is sometimes used to reveal the spiritual condition of the people: barren, unfruitful land mirroring a barren, unfruitful people because they have sinned. The Book of Joel is an example.

Our environmental decay reflects our spiritual degeneracy. But today's green movement is red with the blood of the innocent unborn when it hypocritically puts the saving of snail darters or rain forests ahead of protecting human life. Sadly, many environmentalists support abortion because it serves their agenda. Continuing our duplicity will only hasten our downfall, not save our environment. Good environmentalism starts with repentance—and with the saving of those for whom God created the environment.

Christians concerned about the environment should remember God's promise: "If my people, who are called by my name, will humble themselves and pray and seek my face and turn from their wicked ways, then will I hear from heaven and will forgive their sin, and WILL HEAL THEIR LAND." (Emphasis mine).

Of the playboy, the feminist, and the environmentalist, it could be said as was said of Nineveh by Nahum: "From you . . . has one come forth who plots evil against the Lord and counsels wickedness . . . . Woe to the city of blood, full of lies, full of plunder, never without victims! . . . 'I am against you,' declares the Lord Almighty."[18]

Because of our false standards we are a society that is veering all over the road morally and spiritually. We are prideful and arrogant, yet we spurn correction. Ours is like the society Jesus saw when He approached Jerusalem for the last time. The crowd was jubilant, waving palm branches and placing cloaks on the road. Outwardly it was a triumphant time.

But Jesus knew that in just days the crowd would scream for His crucifixion, and He would go to the cross. Amid the fanfare, Jesus saw the city. And He wept over it. He saw beyond the outwardly happy, festive throng greeting Him. He saw the soul of the city. He saw its sin. And prophetically He saw its tragic collapse when the city would be ravished by the Romans in A.D. 70.

Jesus wept over Jerusalem's sin. He wept in compassion. He wept with grief. He knew that sin separates individuals, people, and nations from God. That was why He had journeyed to Jerusalem—to die for our sin. In Jerusalem, Jesus willingly walked a path of suffering for us. Three special places marked that path: Gethsemane, Gabbatha, and Golgotha. But it was not just the suffering that was significant—it was who was suffering and why!

At the cross, God was very precise about sin. Only the God who hates sin—and loves us—would permit the cross. Whenever we retrace Christ's torturous steps, we should be sobered and sickened at sin—our sin. Looking at our casual, cavalier attitude toward sin in the light of the cross should shake us and grieve us: "This is what my sin brought!"

Our cry of compassion for the world must be filled with the cross. Our voice must be saturated with God's love for this prodigal world and grief over our sin. Those who hear us or watch how we live must see that we know the depth of the meaning and purpose of the cross. With that passion we must raise our voice in the nations!

My dear friend, evangelist Paul Lowenberg, who has spent over fifty years in anointed ministry around the world, spoke passionately of such a voice at a convention attended by 10,000 people, mainly pastors and their wives:

> Christ can only multiply himself through you and me; the spirit of Calvary must be duplicated in ten thousand of God's workers . . . Jesus came weeping, shall we follow Him dry-eyed? . . . He came into

abject poverty . . . shall we seek prosperity and affluence? He came to die . . . shall we seek security and ease? . . . That passion, that dying, that burden, those tears will germinate the seed which week after week and month after month have dropped onto dry, arid soil. Through the cross God provided for us that most beautiful of words: forgiveness. We have one urgency: repentance![19]

When We Are Precise About Sin

Repentance is when we get precise about sin. Repentance is having the grief God has over my sin. It is agreeing with God about evil, calling it what He calls it—sin.

As Arthur Pink said:

> Genuine and saving repentance is taking sides with God against myself . . . repentance is designed to make the heart loathe sin, and that through a deep sense of its infinite enormity and dreadful pollution: it is to make us dread sin through a heart-realization of its awful guilt . . . . Evangelical repentance makes no excuses and has no reserves, but cries "I have dishonored Thy name, grieved Thy Spirit, abused Thy patience."[20]

Such an attitude comes through seeing the cross. Pink said, "Not until we have realized that our rebellion against God was such that nothing but the death of Christ could possibly atone for it, have we truly repented."[21]

In 1750, J. Bellamy said eloquently:

> Repentance stands then in opposition to . . . that sin-extenuating, self-justifying, law-hating, God-blaspheming disposition which reigns in every impenitent soul . . . . [In repentance] we justify God, approve His law, condemn ourselves, accept the

> punishment of our iniquity as worthy of God; and
> thus we confess, repent, and turn unto the Lord,
> looking only to free grace through Jesus Christ for
> pardon.[22]

We're commanded to repent! In Athens, the
Apostle Paul in his famous sermon said, "In the past
God overlooked such ignorance, but now he commands
all people everywhere to repent."[23] When Jesus and
John the Baptist preached "Repent!"[24], it was an
imperative. We're not asked or invited to repent, we're
commanded to repent. There is no apologetic spirit
from God, but an urgent, pressing charge: "Do it!
Now!"

Repentance, however, is not just the action of a
moment, it's the attitude of a lifetime. Have I repented?
Have you? Do we live in a repentant, humble attitude?
Repentance is difficult because it's tough for us to admit
we're wrong, and in our secular society, we don't want
to admit we're accountable to God.

The greatest men and women of God, however,
have been the greatest repenters. One was Ezra. In
chapters nine and ten of his book, Ezra is overwhelmed
with grief because of the sin of the people. So were
others. Their attitude was stirring: "Then everyone who
trembled at the words of the God of Israel gathered
around me because of this unfaithfulness of the exiles.
And I sat there appalled until the evening sacrifice . . .
and fell on my knees with my hands spread out to the
Lord my God and prayed. . . . While Ezra was praying
and confessing, weeping and throwing himself down
before the house of God, a large crowd . . . gathered
around him. They too wept bitterly."[25]

When was the last time you and I trembled at the
words of God? Or were appalled because of sin? Or
fell on our knees with hands lifted? Or wept? Most of
us know what it is to worry about things like being

short of money and lie awake at night thinking about it. But when was the last time we were so concerned about evil in us and in the world, and had such a desire for holiness and for knowing the Lord, that we stayed awake all night on our knees crying out to God?

When the Word of God was read to King Josiah, he expressed deep grief over the sin of Israel and set about to rid the land of idols and the evil practices that were bringing the judgment of God down on the nation.[26] That's repentance!

Repentance for sin must be our public and personal priority. Let the Church lead the way in open, humble and public repentance of our idolatry, our pride, our ignoring God, our immorality, our killing our unborn, and our other violence—all our sins. Let the churches get together to repent and cry out to God for spiritual awakening. Not just once, but again and again. Let them call collective solemn assemblies. It is urgent that it be done now, that it be put ahead of other church programs. It's the one thing that only the Church can do.

Unprecedented, powerful action like that, motivated by the heart of God, will produce a sense of sin in all our surrounding communities—where else but from the Church will our world get such a sense, where else can they see their darkness except in the light of a holy Church? *The world will be precise about sin when the Church is!*

Let the world see the Church weep over the world's sins! Let pastors and priests "weep between the temple porch and the altar"[27] and "spend the night in sackcloth."[28] The world has seen the Church build edifices and ministries. Let it now see the Church go to Gethsemane. Let it see the Church bowed in grief. Let the world hear the Church lift a cry of compassion that is precise about sin.

No other example will be more powerful!
No other example is more needed!

172

[1]Matthew 3:1, 6-8.

[2]John Court, in a public address, Adelaide, Australia, November 25, 1990.

[3](Adelaide, Australia: Axiom Press), p. 30.

[4]John 14:6.

[5]Acts 4:12.

[6]Matthew 7:21.

[7]R. C. Sproul, *Tabletalk,* (Orlando, FL, October 1991), p. 6.

[8]Isaiah 1:4.

[9]Matthew 18:7-9.

[10]Romans 1:29-31.

[11]Isaiah 64:6.

[12]2 Peter 2:22.

[13]Romans 3:13.

[14]Amos 6:1-7.

[15]Amos 4:1-3.

[16]Hosea 4:2b.

[17]Hosea 4:3.

[18]Nahum 1:11; 3:1, 5a.

[19]Paul Lowenberg, address, "The Mandate of the Church," Assemblies of God Council on Evangelism, 1968.

[20]Arthur Pink, (Gospel Mission, Choteau, MT), pp. 24-25.

[21]Ibid., p. 24.

[22]Ibid., p. 18.

[23]Acts 17:30.

[24]Matthew 3:2; 4:17.

[25]Ezra 9:4-5; 10:1.

[26]2 Kings 22 and 23.

[27]Joel 2:17.

[28]Joel 1:13.

12

Clear About Judgment

Let in the light; all sin expose to Christ;
　　whose life no darkness knows.
Before His Cross for guidance kneel;
　　His light will judge and, judging, heal.
　　　　　　　　J. R. Pearcy

I looked upon the world around me as being in
actual rebellion against God . . . that He was mocked,
and scorned, and hated, as when on earth . . . . I came
to realize that . . . the men and women around me in
consequence of their rebellion "were in great danger
of damnation," and "that all of their miseries, present
and to come, were the results of their rebellion against
God."

　　　　　　　　William Booth
　　　　　　　　Founder of the
　　　　　　　　Salvation Army[1]

Once there was a scientist who did research on
fleas. He kept many fleas and trained some of them to
jump on command. He would place them on the table
with one finger nearby, say, "Jump," and over his finger
they would bound. One day he decided to do a special

experiment. So he took several of them and, with tweezers, pulled off two of their six legs from each of them. Then he put them on the table by his finger and ordered them to jump. They struggled, but they jumped. He duly made notes. Then he took the tweezers and pulled off two more legs from each of them. Again he put them on the table by his finger and told them to jump. They really struggled this time, but they valiantly jumped. He made more notes.

A third time he took the tweezers and pulled off each flea's two remaining legs and, as before, put them on the table by his finger. "Jump," he commanded them, but the fleas lay there. He commanded them again, louder, "Jump," but the fleas stayed where they were. Once more in a very loud voice he ordered them, "Jump," but the fleas remained as they were. "Hmmmm," he said. And he wrote in his notebook: "I have discovered that when you pull all six legs off a flea, he becomes deaf!"

We are a society that "pulls the legs off fleas" and then misinterprets—or chooses to disregard—the natural result. Like Israel, we see no connection between moral anarchy and a chaotic society. We lurch from one crisis to another, and we don't see that we're not controlling events any more, they're controlling us—because we are a society out of control. We lie to ourselves. We ignore the truth that the choices we make have consequences.

Proverbs 22:3 says, "A prudent man sees danger and takes refuge, but the simple keep going and suffer for it." We are not prudent. We sin, but we don't give thought to what sin brings. We reject consequences for our sins. We publish pornography and deny that it results in destroyed homes and increased rapes. We kill our unborn because we claim that a woman has the right to choose, then we deny that it harms anyone. Our new social philosophy is that the unborn is a legal nonentity and, therefore, we kill nothing. We deny that the woman's consequent anguish is caused by the abortion she had. We sow death in the womb and try to reap life in society. We will not accept the proposition that releasing inhumanity into the womb has a direct effect on releasing inhumanity in society, that there is a direct connection between the rising violence against the unborn and the rising violence against children and women.

We debauch ourselves willy-nilly and disavow that there are bad effects, somehow presuming that planting weeds gets us strawberries and that cobras make fine house pets. We fall for the same clever lie that Satan used to tempt Adam and Eve when he craftily denied sin's consequence: "You shall not surely die."[2] The seeds of collapse of any society are resident in the sins they permit, but we refuse to accept this in our case.

Take one example: our wanton sexual sin and the explosion in the use of condoms. In a short time, we have seen the condom emerge, dubiously, from crude prophylactic to social savior. This was caused by the two incurable sexually-transmitted diseases, Herpes II and AIDS, that exploded into our culture in the 1980s. In the early 1980s, Herpes II rose like a plague among fornicators and adulterers and homosexuals. There was no cure; once you got it, you always had it. It was viewed as a sort of modern leprosy. Overnight, the generation that had pioneered the sexual revolution was sobered, and the life-style of the free-wheeling one-night stand gave way to more selective sexual sin with partners from whom you might first get a few medical facts. Then entered the condom—wear it and play.

But it was AIDS that brought the condom into its own. If Herpes II sobered us, AIDS shook us, because not only was AIDS incurable, it was fatal—once you got it, you died, no exceptions. AIDS was first transmitted primarily by homosexuals. It still is, but now it has spread so that those involved in heterosexual sin infect others, as do those who share drug needles. And of course AIDS, like Herpes II, hit the innocent babies, spouses, and those getting blood transfusions.

But putting an end to the onslaught of both diseases is simple, just stop the sinful behavior—chastity before marriage and faithfulness during marriage. Instead, we try to head off the disease by telling men and young boys to wear a condom. Wanting to be sinful and safe, they buy the clever lie that using a condom will completely protect them. At the same time, the promoters of condom usage foolishly believe that sexually sinning young people, many who don't clean up their room three days in a row, are going to use a condom every time. If our men and women, and our young boys and girls, continue to get AIDS and die, the judgment will be on a lying society. These are seeds of our own destruction.

Our Chosen Lies

Our self-deception over condoms, however, is only part of the larger lies we have championed, lies that mar and question our judgment. Our living as if God were not there has brought us to damning lies—those lies that we deliberately tell. As *chosen lies*, these are our most serious threat.

Let's look at two passages of Scripture, Romans 1:18-32 and 2 Thessalonians 2:9-12. If any of the Scriptures ought to keep you and me and our society awake at night, these are the ones. In Romans, the phrase "God gave them over" is used three times. This speaks of God withdrawing himself and abandoning determined sinners to their sins and the consequences. In the first use of the phrase, it is giving them over "to sexual impurity" (verse 24). The second use indicates God giving them over "to shameful lusts" (verse 26)—where lesbian and homosexual sin is specified—and "to a depraved mind" (verse 28), followed by a list of sins. The important focus for us is that God gave them over to uncontrollable sin because they willfully chose to reject Him and rebel—to "suppress the truth by their wickedness" (verse 18). Verse 28 is crucial: "Furthermore, since they did not think it worthwhile to retain the knowledge of God, he gave them over to a depraved mind, to do what ought not to be done."

Second Thessalonians 2:10b says, "They perish because they refused to love the truth and so be saved." Verse 12b speaks of those "who have not believed the truth but have delighted in wickedness." Between these two sobering statements is this one: "For this reason God sends them a powerful delusion so that they will believe the lie and so that all will be condemned who have not believed the truth."

What we see is God giving sinners what they stubbornly want. If they defiantly don't want God and determinedly want their sin, then God gives them over to their sin—puts them under its control—and withdraws and abandons them to their iniquity. If they won't love truth, they will get powerful lies. If they don't want the knowledge of God, He'll give them over to a depraved mind.

What about our society? Certainly our secular society does not want the knowledge of God. We haven't wanted the truth, we've preferred to believe lies—clever self-deceptions—because we wanted to sin. We have gotten what we wanted and are reaping the tragic consequences.

As examples, let's look at two lies our society has chosen to believe, lies that have had an immense impact on us, lies that have molded our thinking so extensively that their effect on us could be termed a revolution, lies that are now so entrenched as public dogma that to challenge them is to incur censure. These lies concern two sins: immorality and killing our unborn. Because of these lies we have seared our conscience toward these two evils. Consequently, we have moved ourselves closer to judgment.

The lies are based on the alleged scientific research of Alfred Kinsey and his colleagues on the nature of human sexuality, and on the statistics, slogans, and arguments presented by those who successfully got us to accept abortion on demand. These lies have spawned a sexual revolution in which immorality is so casually condoned that the very fabric of our society is cracking, and the most massive destruction of human life in the history of mankind is taking place through the killing of our unborn.

Immorality and abortion are particularly dangerous because both attack the creation of human life—immorality at the creation, abortion after the creation. Yet both are more and more regarded as morally neutral, and both are increasingly given the status of virtues. For example, live-in fornicators are given the same legal status as married couples, homosexuality is placed alongside male and female as a sexual equal, and abortion is described as a right or compassionate action.

Earlier we looked at the heresies in the pro-choice argument, the dominant one for abortion. Now we need to look back at the earlier deceptions we chose to believe in the first place, the ones that brought us to where we are. In the late 60s and early 70s, pro-abortionists pushed hard for legal abortion-on-demand. In the process, they blatantly used deceit to mold favorable public opinion—they fabricated statistics, some concocted out of thin air, and solemnly presented them to us as facts. In our social and political system, lies to influence community sentiment are never off-limits. Bernard Nathanson, a founder of the National Abortion Rights Action League, but now an intense foe of abortion, chronicled the duplicity in his book, *Aborting America.*

We wanted the legal right to kill our unborn. This was so paramount that we chose—and choose—to believe a lie. We didn't love the truth of God's principle of the sanctity of human life, we didn't want God retained in our knowledge—we arrogantly preferred our own way, so preference replaced principle and we arbitrarily created a new "right." Now a whole generation has been mortally affected; we have killed millions of unborn babies and continue to do so Their blood is on our hands.

George F. Will, in his review of *The Brethren,* a book by Woodward and Armstrong about the United States Supreme Court during the years when Warren Burger was Chief Justice, commented on the court's abortion decision, Roe v. Wade. Apparently the disposition to arbitrarily rule for preconceived views existed:

> The result of that case was never in doubt, and nothing but the result . . . was important to a majority of the Justices . . . an assertion of the woman's right to privacy, but it never was going to be more than pure assertion . . . . The majority believed that liberalized abortions were right and good . . . . The book is a catalogue of result-oriented behavior.[3]

The United States Supreme Court chose to believe a lie, and to impose that lie as state doctrine.

Carl F. H. Henry said:

> Now the West is reverting to its pagan and pre-Christian readiness to murder the innocent and defenseless, to destroy unwanted infants, to dispose of the maimed and the elderly . . . . The fact is that . . . people . . . are moving irrevocably beyond simply the rebellious conscience to a corrupt conscience; one which not only stifles the truth of God and suppresses

the awareness of future judgment, but actually
delights in sin and commends those who practice it.[4]

We also believed the lie about immorality, and are
now reaping what went into the research by Alfred
Kinsey on human sexuality. That research has been
called "a con job on society" by Judith A. Reisman and
Edward W. Eichel in their book, *Kinsey, Sex and Fraud*.[5]
An advertisement for the book pointed to the pervasive
influence of the research on our society so that
"Kinsey's unchallenged conclusions are taught at every
level of education—elementary, high school and
college—and quoted in textbooks as undisputed truth."

Kinsey's report shaped the sexual attitudes, values,
and "what is normal" for a whole generation. It is even
used by many churches to help them counsel single and
married couples. Reisman and Eichel, aided in research
by John Court, charge that the "most famous sex
research project in history was fraudulent."

Reisman and Eichel said, "Because of this fraudulent research, Kinsey's brand of social 'science' has led
to one of the greatest hypocrisies of our time: the
pretense of providing safe-sex instruction to children
while in reality advancing his agenda, including
indulgence in high-risk lifestyles and behaviors."[6]

But again, we refused—and refuse—to love the
truth. We rejected God's happy precepts for sex, and
we didn't want God retained in our knowledge.
Instead, we wanted unrestrained "freedom" to indulge
ourselves in any way we wanted—we "delighted in
wickedness." So when purported "legitimate scientific
research" avowed our lust, we eagerly espoused it. The
debasing impact on our society has almost destroyed
our nation's morality. The essential point, however, is
that we as a society made two pivotal choices based on
lies. We wanted to have what we wanted, so we killed
truth, and we zealously embraced the lies to justify our
having what we wanted to have.

Personally excusing ourselves by saying we didn't know, or hadn't thought it all through, will not let us out of the damning indictment. We each must answer to God. In spite of our self-justification, our fouled choices carry heavy personal and societal consequences. With our sin goes death. Things have become so bad in our nation, that we should ask ourselves the question: "Has God given us over to our degradation, perversions, and depraved minds?"

If we fall, it will be self-inflicted. Phillip Hughes said:

> Sinful man needs no assistance in working out his own perdition. Ungodliness unaided brings its own judgment on man and society here and now, in addition to final judgment hereafter. To be given up by God to wallow in the filth of one's own making is itself self-manufactured judgment.[7]

In the British Parliament in April, 1990, during a debate over fetal experimentation, MP Patrick Duffy said, "How we treat human life at any of its stages is of the highest moral significance . . . we stand in danger of creating a society that is potentially self-destructive."[8]

Needed—A Word From God

Western society is now at a crossroads, a watershed moment. The days ahead will be a time of accountability for our choices. Right now we desperately need a word from God; our survival depends on it. We need a clear word, unclouded by fads and false prophets, that distinctly articulates our situation. That word should come from the Church, but the Church seems uncertain of her role—even of what is right and wrong. Nicols Fox observed, "It isn't the churches. It's not so much that their moral leadership is being ignored as that, to a great extent, they've abdicated that role. Collectively they seem to exude the same relativism and insecurity about right and wrong as the rest of us. The fact is, we all have a pretty good idea of what is right and wrong, but deprived—as the twentieth century is— of the ever-handy threat of Judgment Day, we just can't seem to find a good enough explanation for why we should do one thing and not another."[9]

We have stripped the twentieth century of concern about Judgment Day. Over fifty years ago, H. Richard Niebuhr decried distortion of the Gospel: "A God without wrath brought men without sin into a kingdom without judgment through the ministrations of a Christ without a Cross."[10] Today's false prophets add to our confusion. Church historian Martin Marty saw a decline in the belief in hell among contemporary Christians and said that it might not be a bad thing: "I have no doubt that the passing of hell from modern consciousness . . . is one of the major if still largely undocumented modern trends."[11]

The trend is not new. Some 250 years ago, in perhaps the most famous sermon ever preached in America, "Sinners in the Hands of an Angry God," Jonathan Edwards said, "Almost every natural man that hears of hell, flatters himself that he shall escape it."

As reported in *USA Today*, contemporary church-men are assuring us that "AIDS isn't God's wrath."[12] The report continued, "Almost universally, whether liberal or conservative, the groups are saying it's bad theology to say this is a judgment of God . . . .' Almost no one today believes God singles out individuals or groups for special punishment in their lifetimes. God doesn't work like that."[13] That's pretty assured speaking, telling us how God won't work or what isn't His wrath. The false prophets in Jeremiah's day also had that assured tone just before Jerusalem fell.

Today's false prophets give little or no mention that

AIDS exploded through homosexual perversion, and that the deadly infection continues to be spread primarily through sinful sexual behavior and through sharing drug needles, ignoring the conclusion that AIDS might—just might—be the consequence of sin.

Is AIDS the judgment of God? R. C. Sproul said: "The Bible makes it clear that God punishes sin. There can be no doubt that infectious diseases like syphilis, gonorrhea and AIDS are Divine punishments for fornication. It is amazing to observe news commentators and liberal Christian spokespeople who deny this."[14] Concerning questions about judgment, one reason we continually come up with wrong answers is because we persist in asking the wrong questions, such as, "Will a loving God send anyone to hell?" This subtly impugns the character of God. A better question: "Considering the enormity of our sin, why aren't we in hell now?" Why don't we ask questions of that kind? Are we afraid of the answers?

Another reason for wrong answers is that we have fashioned a god in our image. This god is a stripped-down model—only forgiving and loving and nice, not holy or just or wrathful. We have carefully selected the characteristics that suit us, that are perfect for our secular mind set. To develop a god we like, and that likes us, we have eliminated accountability, judgment, omnipotence, sovereignty, total knowledge, and omnipresence. But such a god, as we have seen, is no god at all. That god doesn't exist; it is an idol of our lustful desires and imagination.

But, sadly, today's secular god has become the god of many churches. Under the delusion that we need a *here-and-now-god* in order to reach a secular society that thinks primarily in the present tense, many churches have packaged a modern god that will be acceptable to sinning humans. He is a nearby, friendly, buddy-god that exists solely to meet our physical needs and solve our problems, to makes us feel good, and to show us how to be successful and happy. As a result, several biblical topics for sermons have had to be laid aside— sin, guilt, judgment, punishment, an eternal hell, repentance, righteousness, holiness, an eternal heaven. What kind of converts does such a god produce? The kind many churches are getting—unrepentant, unholy, and worldly.

Over the centuries, preaching has swung between God's wrath and God's love. With the former, there was also sometimes harshness and legalism—with the latter, there was sometimes permissiveness and antinomianism, which we are seeing today. But wrath and love are not mutually exclusive, they both are in the character of God and they interrelate. William Eisenhower said, "Preachers of an earlier era reassured their listeners that the wrath of God was conditioned by His love. It falls to us to assert that the latter is conditioned by the former."[15] He also said something startling:

> We can believe in a "God" acceptable to culture, a "God" of all-accepting, morally indifferent, unconditional love, or we can repent and believe in the God of the Old and New Testaments. But we cannot do both. They are incompatible. It is time to awaken, to strengthen what remains, and to reopen our eyes to what the Bible actually says.[16]

The Bible tells that there is accountability for sin, there is judgment. But this has become almost a lost element in modern preaching and teaching. It's as if a whole portion of the Word of God doesn't exist, such as Jesus' warning, "Unless you repent, you too will all perish,"[17] or Paul's admonition, "Do not be deceived: God cannot be mocked. A man reaps what he sows."[18]

The Scriptures wonderfully proclaim the mercy and love of God, and sometimes we have drawn from this the unwarranted conclusion that God is so merciful as to be devoid of justice, and so loving as to be incapable of anger. But the Scriptures also proclaim that "our God is a consuming fire,"[19] and that He will be as resolute in punishment of the persistently wicked—such as Sodom and Gomorrah—as He will be gracious in sparing the repentant—such as Nineveh. Proportionate to His immeasurable justice to the unrepentant sinner is His immeasurable patience to the struggling repentant.

God's view is different from ours. God's clock does not measure days and years, it measures events and necessities. That measure includes the law of sowing and reaping, which means that the seed we sow today will bear its fruit tomorrow. Retribution is the natural fruit of sin. Our wise and gracious Lord and God has constructed His universe on the principle that every form of rebellion shall bear in itself the seed of penalty. The pivot on which everything turns is righteousness. As dynamite is by nature explosive and, if lit, will explode, so our sin is, by its character, destructive and can bring only destruction. As love unites and bonds, so iniquity divides and decays.

The Church *must* take the warnings of the Scriptures seriously. If the Church doesn't, who will? Herbert Schlossberg said, "Human actions have moral consequences. There is a principle of moral accountability in the universe. Idolatry destroys those who indulge themselves in it. One of the prophets of the northern kingdom put it this way: 'With their silver and gold they made idols for their own destruction' (Hosea 4:8). This connection between idolatry and retribution means that people who allow themselves to be seduced by idols seek to solve their problems by finding solutions to what will prove disastrous."[20]

Equitable justice will be meted out. Never yet has God failed to vindicate His righteousness. Never yet have transgressors escaped, and never will they. As certain as sunshine, vengeance will come. Wrath accumulates as in a thundercloud and is poured out when the storm breaks out.

Today as the thundercloud forms, the Church must see the significance of our nation's moral condition, see the moral and spiritual aspect of its injustice and immorality, and fearlessly and compassionately speak up. The Church's cry of compassion must be filled with the reality of judgment.

In speaking up, the Church should remember that unrepentant society and individuals will delude themselves to the very last, buoying themselves up with false hopes that they can escape judgment. So the message of the Church needs to speak to the heart and conscience, probing them deeply and precisely before God.

After votes in the British Parliament "broadened the availability of abortion" and "allowed experimentation on human embryos," Lyndon Bowring and Charlie Cochester of CARE in London wrote, "We believe these parliamentary votes were a national disaster. Something died within us as we recognized that our society had taken a major step towards the darkness of secular humanism."

Bowring and Cochester then addressed the nation's conscience: "We stand before an awesome God. If, as a nation, gross injustice is habitually inflicted on the weakest and most vulnerable of our community, the unborn and the handicapped, what can we expect? Parliament weighed God's principle of the sanctity of human life and came down in favor of man's desire for the quality of life. We see it as inevitable that there will soon be major pressure to legalize both infanticide and euthanasia." In this address, they quoted from Daniel 5:27: "You have been weighed in the balance and found wanting."

This is the kind of message the Church must speak

to a prideful culture of killing that has a bloodstain as big as the whole earth. With human justice hidden away, the Church must confront a society willfully deluded by clever lies while the blood of millions of destroyed unborn children cries out for God's judgment. If we are convinced of our nation's sin and of God's righteousness, we must be equally convinced of our nation's judgment "because the land is full of bloodshed and the city is full of violence."[21]

Our nation now faces the rule of retribution: "The day is here! It has come! Doom has burst forth, the rod has budded, arrogance has blossomed! Violence has grown into a rod to punish wickedness."[22] Our nation's violence—our killing—will grow into a rod to punish our wickedness.

Our sins are so extensive that it is now as Amos said to the six pagan nations, "God will not turn back His wrath." All mankind is now caught in the vortex of swiftly accelerating crises when every crisis could be our last. The cracks are already in the dam, and they are rapidly widening and water is pouring through. Even in the face of this, our secular society heedlessly continues to say to God the words of the wicked that Job spoke about: "Leave us alone! We have no desire to know your ways."[23]

Will our nation get what it wants?

Our Nation's Crisis Should Affect the Agenda of the Church

Our situation should drive us to our knees in repentance. The prospect of judgment must affect the agenda of the Church, its message, its programs, its plans. The Church must give priority to raising its voice in the streets of our modern Nineveh. We must not, like Jonah, run the other way and sail for Tarshish instead of delivering God's message to the wicked "city of blood." That's what Nahum, the prophet, called Nineveh, the magnificent capital of the Assyrian nation[24]—and it surely is what God is calling our nation today. Nineveh had only forty days before judgment would destroy them completely, yet the prophet ran from his commission to proclaim God's Word to them.

Jonah's ship of escape was shaken by a fierce storm that was so destructive that only throwing the prophet overboard saved it. In recent years, there has been shaking in the Church, with the signs of it being the fall of some well-known televangelists and many relatively unknown ministers. Could God be shaking us about our priorities, and our message—and where and when that message is to be proclaimed? Are success, selfishness, personal happiness, prosperity, and a myriad of fads really the saving messages for our nation's time of impending judgment? Is not any preaching that constantly avoids sin, judgment, repentance, and holiness no more than our ships of escape from our Nineveh? Jonah, by running, said, "Nineveh, I don't care about you; go ahead into damnation!" Are we saying the same thing with our sidetracking sermons?

It took three days of prayer in the stomach of a fish for Jonah to get it sorted out with God. From that belly of Sheol, Jonah cried to God and pledged: "What I have vowed I will make good."[25] After the fish vomited him out, Jonah heard again the Lord's command to go to Nineveh with His message. This time he went. God's message that Jonah preached in Nineveh was to the point: "Forty more days and Nineveh will be overturned."[26]

It was a message of judgment. But it had an incredible, forceful, and redeeming effect. From peasant to king, the city repented in sackcloth, and a sweeping spiritual awakening broke out in Nineveh. It was one of the greatest spiritual awakenings in history.

Jonah proclaimed God's message of judgment. But what if Jonah had substituted his own wisdom for God's and gone into Nineveh with a positive "peace, peace," feel-good proclamation? What if he had held a seminar on prosperity, or a campaign on how to be happy and get your needs met, or a conference on success, or preached a hundred other fashionable and socially acceptable messages? Jonah probably would have gotten a huge crowd, he probably would have gotten the king and community leaders to come—but the nation would have gone into judgment even as Jonah was preaching to his big crowds and the social and national leaders. The king would never have humbled himself and issued his wholehearted call to repentance. That kind of repentant response comes only when God's message for the moment is preached. We must decide whether we want to tickle ears or penetrate hearts, whether we want a crowd or a revival, whether we want to fill offering plates or fill heaven.

The edict of the king of Nineveh was urgent: "Let everyone call urgently on God. Let them give up their evil ways and their violence. Who knows? God may yet relent and with compassion turn from his fierce anger so that we will not perish."[27] He was right. The heavenly Father graciously answered this prayer and they did not perish: "When God saw what they did and how they turned from their evil ways, he had compassion and did not bring upon them the destruction he had threatened."[28]

Though a reluctant prophet, Jonah was a true prophet; he warned, he spoke God's message clearly without compromise, and he told the people of Nineveh what they needed to hear—what God wanted them to hear. Having heard the message from God from a prophet sent by God, all of Nineveh repented and turned from their wickedness.

During the Civil War, Abraham Lincoln called for

a day of fasting and prayer to seek the Lord. He said, "Sometimes it seems necessary that we should be confronted with perils which threaten us with disaster in order that we may not get puffed up and forget Him."[29] Lincoln saw the war bringing judgment and said, "Every drop of blood drawn with the lash shall be paid by the sword." The Civil War was a watershed moment for the United States—it could have meant the end of the Union. But Lincoln's and the nation's repentance was strategic and in time. It would be glory on earth if the president and prime minister of every nation today would follow the example of Abraham Lincoln and the king of Nineveh and issue a similar call to repentance. But if they did, the people would probably laugh them out of office.

Was Jonah happy over Nineveh's repentance and God's mercy? No. But even his angry response to God contained a beautiful description of our Lord's character: "I knew that you are a gracious and compassionate God, slow to anger and abounding in love, a God who relents from sending calamity."[30] And the last sentence of the Book of Jonah is a question from God's heart: "Should I not be concerned about that great city?"[31] True compassion is always clear about judgment and warns those who are about to be judged.

In Nineveh, there was sin and rebellion that demanded to be judged, yet the Father cared deeply for the people of Nineveh. His compassion sent Jonah to them with a message of coming judgment, and it brought repentance and revival. Isn't this what we want today?

Is there anything greater that the Church should want?

---

[1] William Booth, quoted in *The Anglo-Saxon Tradition*, by George Catlin, (Broadway House, London, 1939), p. 191.
[2] Genesis 3:4.

[3] George F. Will, (*Newsweek*, December 10, 1979), p. 140.

[4] Carl F. H. Henry, *Religious Broadcasting*, April 1983, p. 25.

[5] Judith A. Reisman and Edward W. Eichel, *Kinsey, Sex and Fraud*, (Lafayette, LA: Huntington House, 1990).

[6] From ad for *Kinsey, Sex and Fraud*.

[7] Phillip Hughes, *Christians in a Secular Society*, (Baker Book House, Grand Rapids, MI), from an ad for the book.

[8] Patrick Duffy, MP, quoted in *CARE News* (No. 27, 1990).

[9] Nicols Fox, *Newsweek*, (February 13, 1989), p. 8.

[10] H. Richard Niebuhr, quoted in *Christianity Today*, (March 20, 1987), p. 26.

[11] *The Oregonian*, (Portland, OR, Saturday, April 26, 1986).

[12] *USA Today*, September 22, 1989.

[13] Ibid.

[14] R. C. Sproul, *Tabletalk*, May, 1991, p. 18.

[15] William Eisenhower, "Sleepers in the Hands of an Angry God," (*Christianity Today*), p. 28.

[16] Ibid.

[17] Luke 13:3, 5.

[18] Galatians 6:7.

[19] Hebrews 12:29.

[20] Herbert Schlossberg, *Idols for Destruction*, (Nashville, TN: Thomas Nelson, 1983), p. 293.

[21] Ezekiel 7:23.

[22] Ezekiel 7:10-11.

[23] Job 21:14.

[24] Nahum 3:1.

[25] Jonah 2:9.

[26] Jonah 3:4.

[27] Jonah 3:8-9.

[28] Jonah 3:10.

[29] Abraham Lincoln, quoted in *Our Dance Has Turned to Death* (Atlanta, GA: Renewal Publishing Co.), p. 6.

[30] Jonah 4:2.

[31] Jonah 4:11.

13

God's Dream for Fathers

Children crying in the night,
Children crying for the light,
And with no language but a cry.
                    C. Clemance[1]

As a young man, I was deeply affected by what the great English preacher, Charles Spurgeon, wrote to his son, "I should not like you, if meant by God to be a missionary, to die a millionaire. I should not like it, were you fitted to be a missionary, that you should drivel down to be a king." Then Spurgeon placed it in perspective:

> What are all your kings, all your nobles, all your diadems, when you put them together, compared with the dignity of winning souls to Christ; with the special honor of building for Christ, not on another man's foundation, but preaching Christ's Gospel in the regions far beyond.

There is beautiful spiritual truth in what Spurgeon wrote, but beyond saying that about his words, we should exclaim about Spurgeon himself: "What a father!" Those are wonderfully inspiring words from a father to his son. I wonder what Spurgeon's son did with them? Did he know that he had a treasure in a father who spoke to him with such vision?

But it is not the eloquence of words that is attractive in these words of Spurgeon—although not many of us can express ourselves as poignantly as Spurgeon—it is the eloquence of a father's heart.

That is today one of the most widespread, deep-seated yearnings in our nation—to know a father's heart. It is essential to the well-being of our nation that we begin to raise up godly, caring fathers. As I said in a previous chapter, many of the sins ravaging our society are primarily male sins: rape, pornography, molestation, pedophilia, drugs, violence, homosexual perversion, etc.

If an errant manhood is our defining delinquency, then a revived manhood—with renewed fathers in particular—is our defining answer. That means grandfathers, also. Good men, good fathers, good grandfathers, and even good great-grandfathers are the answer to all of our nation's social problems.

However, while most men may want to be good fathers, there are many times that it is difficult for a man to be one. John Smith, an Australian Gospel minister, may have discerned one of the reasons for that difficulty. His observation on the Australian male is one that could be written about men almost anywhere in the West: "Men in Australia are suffering from cosmic orphanhood. We have a lack of the sense of being properly fathered, so we have no idea of the true nature of fatherhood. As a nation of husbands and fathers we tend to be hopelessly irresponsible, and the women are left to carry the load."[2]

Smith's commentary of "cosmic orphanhood" and "a lack of the sense of being properly fathered," suggests that most fathers themselves have been fatherless at least emotionally, if not physically. If true, this signals great troubles today for manhood, troubles that fundamentally affect society.

It is fortunate, therefore, that God already has the solution to the "cosmic orphanhood" problem. The most helpful and powerful place that fatherless fathers (who are struggling to become true fathers) can go for help is to the Father of us all, Almighty God—I learned this from personal experience. If those who are or are going to be fathers would learn to go to their heavenly Father for help, we would see develop a generation of godly men who know God; men who "are so tall when they pray, that when they get down on their knees they reach clear into heaven"; men who are secure in their masculinity and have accepted responsibility for their sexual drive; men who openly love their wives and children and are leading their families to God under the guidance of the Holy Spirit. Sounds simplistic and idealistic—but the revolutionary effect of such men would turn our nation upside down and make it right-side up. The impact these men would have as role models for our young men and women—and even our children—would be immeasurable. Our society needs a mighty spiritual awakening—and we would have one if godly men like these rose up as a new generation of fathers.

God has such a dream for manhood.

Part of God's dream for a godly man, particularly a husband and a father, is that he learn to love:

> Husbands, love your wives, just as Christ loved
> the church and gave himself up for her to make her
> holy, cleansing her by the washing with water
> through the word, and to present her to himself as a
> radiant church . . . . In this same way, husbands ought
> to love their wives as their own bodies. He who loves

> his wife loves himself . . . . Each one of you must love
> his wife as he loves himself."[3]

In this excerpt from Ephesians, love is mentioned seven times. Integral to God's vision for a man is that he love openly, expressively, joyously. Certainly most of us men have no trouble with the *concept* of being *able* to love, and we believe that we can do it—at least in our thoughts and our imaginations. But many of us have trouble in actually doing what we believe we are capable of doing. In fact, most men know acutely the intense discomfort of wanting to verbally express love to a loved one, but not being able to get the right words out in the right way.

Some are like a man John Smith described: "I remember going to see a man who was very depressed, quite close to suicide, whose wife had just gone after another man. He simply stated, 'My wife's left me.' I asked him why. 'I don't know why,' he said. 'She says I don't love her, that I'm only interested in sex.' Then he shuddered with a deep sense of anguish, and in desperation he looked up at me and shook his head and said, 'I don't know any other way to show love, except sex.'"[4]

It may well be because of the fathering we've had, or the influences we had growing up, or just because our personality developed in the way that it did, that we find it tough to feel and express tender love. In fact, it could be that learning to love is the toughest thing that we tough men will ever have to do. And the first thing we need to learn is that if we have a hang-up in being able to freely communicate love, we didn't get it from God. God's on our side in all this. He wants us to be loving men, loving fathers, loving grandfathers, and loving great-grandfathers. In fact, that's what He created us to be; we just managed to get messed up somewhere along the way. Where, doesn't matter. It's not going to solve our problem—and it never solves any problem—to try to find someone or something that we can point our finger at and blame for the way we are. What we need to do is take hold of our spiritual bootstraps and get on with God's plan for us as men and fathers.

Let's start with how we can learn to really love.

We start by learning from the heavenly Father through the example of our Savior: We are to love our wives "as Christ loved the church and gave himself up for her." This is sacrificial, self-giving, other-person love. A husband who has trouble verbalizing his love to his wife should begin to openly exhibit an attitude of *sacrificial love* for her. This is a love that gives to her, that does things for her, that goes out of its way to help her, that makes life easier for her, that expresses concern for the way she feels, that is interested in what she thinks and does; love that makes her the center of life, the joy of life, the pleasure of life and the interest of life. Make this a life-style and the words expressing the new attitude of love will soon follow.

Difficult? Probably. Worth it? Immeasurably so!—both in blessing to the wife and in personal fulfillment.

Now look at Christ's purpose in loving the Church and sacrificing himself for it: "To present her to himself as a radiant church." That's why Christ did it, so that He would have a radiant Church. Men should know happily that there is a special cosmetic that only a husband can give his wife. She can have access to the very choicest beauty aids from the finest salons, but there is one cosmetic she can receive only from her husband: RADIANCE. She receives that from the tenderness, security, and joy of her husband's love. A radiant woman is always a beautiful woman. When a husband loves his wife as Christ loved the Church, he makes his wife beautiful by releasing from within her that ultimate radiance that only a godly and loving woman married to a godly and loving husband can have. As the husband loves, so will the wife, for love begets love.

God's dream for a man includes being a role model, a teacher—a hero—to his children: "Fathers, do not exasperate your children," the Scripture says, "instead, bring them up in the training and instruction of the Lord."[5] Again, this is difficult, because most men find it difficult to really train and instruct their children in the Lord, while they do know the experience of exasperating them. Part of the problem may be that many men may not be training and instructing themselves in the ways of the Lord. So they should begin there and determine to know God and His ways and make Him the center of their lives.

As fathers, we teach our children, good or bad, whether we say anything to them or not. One of the primary lessons we teach them is PRIORITIES—WHAT IS IMPORTANT AROUND OUR HOUSE. If your heart is after God and your children see you with that priority, it lets them know that their dad has a heart after the Lord—THAT AROUND THEIR HOUSE, KNOWING GOD IS IMPORTANT. "But as for me and my household, we will serve the Lord."[6] Such an example is powerful. A father with a heart after God will find the Lord wonderfully enabling him to instruct his children.

The man learning to love his wife and instruct his children should set three goals for his family:

- A wife who is radiant.
- Sons who whistle.
- Daughters who sing.

These are the same goals the heavenly Father has for His children. He wants us joyful and alive, exulting in life. The sound of our joy is beautiful to His ears.

Men should want to hear the same from their children.

To help give their sons and daughters such exuberance, men should instruct them in celebrating life and love—teach them that life is a gift from God, and that it is beautiful and sacred. They should help them to be gripped and inspired by the wonder and majesty of life as God has given it, help them to be captured by the idyllic, help them to look up on a cloudless night and be awed by the magnitude of God's universe, help them to stand on a mountainside on a bright day and be stirred by the grandeur of God's earth. This is also something that grandparents should do with their grandchildren. In the plan of God, grandparents are to be in the vanguard of transferring the mature values of life and love to the younger generation.

Parallel to the sweeping effect a revived manhood would have on our society would be that of revived grandparents. Their impact on the younger generations would be profound. In a society that worships youth, it is difficult sometimes to feel needed; but grandparents are greatly needed—needed by our nation and needed by God to help train the younger generations in the way that they should go.

Margaret Barclay wrote,

> Teenagers go off the rails because parents are too busy grabbing dollars for material well-being to bother about their offspring or even their own parents . . . . A nation neglects the caring and wisdom of the old at its peril . . . . Bring back the grandparents."[7]

Instructing in the Facts of Life

For men and grandparents to give their children and grandchildren that celebration of life, they need to instruct them happily in the real facts of life. Those facts include three things we need to know about ourselves and for which we must accept responsibility.

First, our God-given identity. Let them know that human life started with a dream—God's dream. "So God created man in his own image, in the image of God he created him."[8] Our creation was a creation of ultimate excellence, as God took His own image and reproduced it in us—creatures created specially for Him. In the hand of God, the dust of the earth was transformed into a man, and God "breathed into his nostrils the breath of life, and the man became a living being."[9]

That's how we began. Our character reflected the image of our Creator. We were given a moral image, the power of choice and a free will; an intellectual image, the capacity to learn, explore and discover; a creative image, the ability to design, build and invent things from architecture to art; an emotional image, the capacity for love and joy; a spiritual image, the ability to know God; and an eternal image, the possession of an immortal soul.

Each of us is an unrepeatable miracle! Every conception that gave every human being life was, and remains, a once-in-a-universe occurrence—never had it happened before, never will it happen again. Each of us is a rarity of one, a singular masterpiece into which the creative excellence of almighty God has been poured.

Second, our God-given sexuality. Not only did God create us in His image, but He also created us male and female: "So God created man in his own image, in the image of God he created him; male and female he created them."[10]

You may ask me who I am, and I might respond by saying I am a husband, or a father, or a minister, or whatever. However, these are not who I am, they are only roles I fill. One of the biggest problems most of us have as men is that of confusing what we do with who we are. We tend to define ourselves by what we do.

Who am I? I am a male person made in the image of God—so is every other man—only my physical appearance is different from that of all other men. In the same way, if you are a woman, you are a female person made in the image of God; only your physical appearance is different from that of all other women. Our sexuality, the difference between men and women, has to do with our total character as we were created by God in His image.

When the distinctions between male and female are being blurred and distorted tragically, this is especially important for our young people and children to understand—they are special young men and women, young boys and girls, made in the image of God. All parents need to pray much for their children that God will open their hearts and minds to the knowledge and certainty of who they are.

Third, our God-given fertility. In His creation of human beings, God had a very extraordinary gift to bestow. The heavens He created would not possess it, the plant life would not, the insect life would not, the fish life would not, the animals of the land would not. Only human beings would. The gift from God would so uniquely express God's essential character of life that human beings would be the only creatures who could receive it, for human beings alone possess God's moral, intellectual, and spiritual imprint. The gift would be a love gift because only human beings have the capacity to love. The gift would be a dream gift because only human beings have the ability to dream. The gift would be a choice gift because only human beings have the power to choose. The gift would be a personal gift because only human beings have the potential for intimacy. What is this special gift? *It is the ability to procreate life by an act of will.* Scripture says, "God blessed them and said to them, 'Be fruitful and increase in number; fill the earth and subdue it.'"[11]

Human beings alone have the capacity to conceive

life by choice, by an act of volition, by wanting to. Animals reproduce, but they do so by instinct. Their internal programming, put there by God, dictates when they mate, conceive, and bear young. But not human beings. Our gift is unique. We choose when to bring forth new life.

God created the first life. Then He gave human beings the ability to reproduce life in cooperation with Him, to procreate by will. God didn't give this capacity to one will, but to two wills, a male will and a female will; and He designed a wonderful plan whereby one male-will and one female-will come together in a special relationship of lifelong, committed love called marriage. In the beautiful, exclusive, sacred, physical intimacy of their marriage, they would have one will. In this one will of intimacy, they would have the capacity for procreating another life also made in God's image. Man and woman alone have such God-given fertility. It is wondrous beyond imagination.

God's plan is so special that He expects us never to express our fertility except within the bonds of marriage, and exclusively with the one person to whom we are committed for life. No exceptions. Our fertility is something for which we should accept responsibility before we date or marry.

Study these facts in the Holy Spirit's light and teach them to your children and grandchildren so that they may see the false promises of immorality—the deceptions that ultimately pervert, cheapen, and enslave the sexuality of men and women and turn the promise of love into lust, the promise of pleasure into license, the promise of understanding into insensitivity, the promise of liberation into bondage.

A father can have no greater joy than when his children celebrate life as God intended them to—when his sons whistle and his daughters sing. In God, his children will have roots to stabilize them and wings so they can fly.

To Men and Grandparents

There are several things that all Christian men and grandparents should do.

To both men and grandparents. First, support the children and teenagers in our churches with prayer and encouragement, and teach them through words and actions how to live a biblically moral life. We must go beyond telling them the truth of living for Christ and show them the proof of the benefits of righteousness, and exhibit the joy of life in Christ. As men and grandparents, we must celebrate His life before them.

Second, when there is immorality or abortion within our church, we must confront the sin with compassion. We must call for repentance and renunciation of the sin and when the call is heeded, we must offer the redeemed sinner loving arms of acceptance and forgiveness.

Third, we must call the Church to accountability and action. Too long we've merely ignored or doled out condemnation when confronted with our culture's sins. Instead, we must begin to offer genuine help, concrete answers, and viable alternatives to those struggling with moral dilemmas.

Fourth, we must sound the warning of God's impending judgment on our society in the face of its continuing sin. We must make it clear that without repentance we face God's judgment. God's desire is not to judge and destroy, but to forgive and heal our world, our countries, our communities, our churches—each individual.

Fifth, we need to lead the way in intercession for our families, our churches and our nation. Read Ezekiel 22 again. Then reread it, let it stir you. Pray by name for your spouse and for each child or grandchild. Pray for pastors and family by name, and for elders, deacons and others in spiritual leadership in your church. Pray for your national and local leaders—the president, prime minister, members of parliament and legislature. Pray for the nation. Pray much for revival in the Church and for spiritual awakening in the community. Pray that the voice of the Church will be raised today, both in intercessory prayer and in bold proclamation of the Gospel of the Kingdom of God. If you believe we are in terminal days and that our sins are massive and we are headed for judgment, then stand before the Lord in the gap in intercession.

Sixth, look at our world through the eyes of Christ. Have His and the heavenly Father's cry of compassion.

To grandparents. First, recognize that God has an absolutely vital, beautiful ministry for you. Though you may retire from active employment, there is no retirement age in our Lord's plan; rather, this is an opportunity for the Lord's work. Make it a matter of prayer.

Second, as mentioned earlier, do step forward in transferring the values of life to your grandchildren, and to the children and teenagers of your church and neighborhood. Whatever their age, tell them they are special, made in God's image, boy or girl, and that you are praying for them. Become a strong encourager. Your encouragement will have a powerful impact on the child or teenager. No matter how they look or act outwardly, your word of affirmation in a put-down world will be one of the most powerful statements they will ever hear. Do it!

Third, be strongly involved in the spiritual support of your local church and pastor. Be visible at times of prayer. Step forward when there is an altar response. From the maturity of your Christian experiences, you know the way the enemy works; so take authority in spiritual warfare.

To men. First, we must confess to Christ any sin of immorality within our own lives—whether it be adultery for the husband, or illicit sex for the single male, or pornography. Above all, the sinning must stop! If married, we must determine under God to be "the husband of but one wife," which includes being a man focused on his wife, with eyes only for her, a one-woman man.

Second, we must support one another with prayer and encouragement, getting together with other Christian men. We must endeavor to live as Christ commanded—being a living witness in our community. Older men especially, be a strong encourager to younger men. Your affirmation of them carries weight. Help them to be godly in their relationships with young women. They need the help. In today's moral climate, young men in their relationships toward women, as one observer put it, "are encouraged to pick any peach on the tree, and if you come upon a pit, you can pitch it."

Third, we must support our wives and the single women in our churches with prayer and encouragement.

Fourth, be a man involved. You are needed. The times are too dangerous for you to sit on the sidelines as a spectator. Ask the Lord where He wants to use you.

Fifth, we need to know God, His character, His Word, His heart. For instance, read Isaiah 6:1-9, a text we examined earlier. Then reread it. Let Isaiah's mighty, magnificent experience become yours. Be a man—and a father—with a heart after God!

I pray that as men we'll all move forward to be the men God dreams for us to be; and that we'll move forward purposefully to protect the fatherless, be anchors for our families, and be backbones for our communities and nation. With God's help, let's be men of prayer and priests in our homes. Through repentance and intercession, let's lead our communities, our cities, and our nation in a spiritual awakening. In the face of the forces that are destroying homes and nations, we must not flinch before the forces of the enemy, but advance resolutely under God, holding high the standard of our Lord Jesus Christ.

> So shall they fear The name of the Lord from the west,
> And His glory from the rising of the sun;
> When the enemy comes in like a flood,
> The Spirit of the Lord will lift up a standard against him.[12]

We live in a day of little men, like pornographers who excrete filth into the public mind and abortionists who without conscience kill our unborn. American newsman and broadcaster Paul Harvey said, "The sun is going down when little men cast long shadows."

As Christian men, let us determine in Christ's name to stand tall.

---

[1] C. Clemance, *Revelation of St. John the Divine*, *Pulpit Commentary* (Eerdmans, Grand Rapids, MI, 1950), p. 19.

[2] John Smith, *Advance Australia*, p. 121.

[3] Ephesians 5:25-33.

[4] Smith, p. 121.

[5] Ephesians 6:4.

[6] Joshua 24:15.

[7] Margaret Barclay, letter to the editor, *The Advertiser*, (Adelaide, Australia, Dec. 1989).

[8] Genesis 1:27.

[9] Genesis 2:7.

[10] Genesis 1:27.

[11] Genesis 1:28.

[12] Isaiah 59:19 (NKJV).

14

Churches God Uses

> Arise, shine, for your light has come, and the glory
> of the Lord rises upon you. See, darkness covers the
> earth and thick darkness is over the peoples, but the
> Lord rises upon you and his glory appears over you.
> Nations will come to your light, and kings to the
> brightness of your dawn.[1]

Years ago, a well-known minister became pastor of
a congregation in a large city. In one of his first
meetings he said to the elders, "Gentlemen, when did
you last have a revival here?"

They answered, "Oh, pastor, we haven't had a
revival in years. In fact, we don't believe in revivals;
we believe the days of revivals are past."

The new pastor looked the elders in the face and
said, "We're either going to have a revival in this
church, or we're going to have a funeral in the
parsonage!"[2]

Our friend Paul Lowenberg shared this story. He
added a fervent observation:

> When men get this desperate, ladies and gentle-
> men, something begins to happen. When we're

willing to secure a revival with blood, with a death certificate, with sweat and tears . . . Whether as a church, or as a nation, or as an individual, when we cease to bleed we cease to bless. Let me ask you, is there blood in our sermon preparation? Is there blood in our prayers? Is there blood in our preaching? Is there blood in our altar calls?[3]

What passion Lowenberg communicated for revival and missions and evangelism. Are we this desperate? We desperately need revival in the Church, a revival that brings a spiritual awakening in society. Why don't we have one? Richard Halverson, Chaplain of the United States Senate, pointed to the lack of desire for a revival in the Church, singling out the secularism and materialism among Christians:

Generally speaking, the people of God are living to get as much as they can out of life this side of the grave . . . . I think you would find very few longing for the return of Christ. His return now would instead constitute an interruption in our plans.

As a result, there is . . . no real longing for an "awakening." God is sovereign in all these things, but to the extent that conditions have to be met for God to send an awakening like the past revivals, I think all the conditions have been met except one: the desire on the part of God's people for an awakening that would issue in righteousness, in selflessness, and in authentic piety."[4]

Of all the compelling, correct reasons that might be marshaled to urge our seeking the Lord for revival, there is one reason that is especially crucial—our young people have not seen revival. Some of us have seen revival, some of the previous generation have seen revival, but our children have not. Jack Hayford, pastor of the Church on the Way in Van Nuys, California, said, "I am deeply concerned. Why? Because we stand at the beginning of the third generation of our movement. Any candid observation of Church history will point to the fact that this is a crisis generation." Hayford then quoted William Fisher, the renowned Nazarene minister, who said, "The most tragic time in the life of any church is when the vision is being carried out by those who never saw it."[5]

This situation provides a special, vital mandate for any grandparents who have experienced a revival in the Church to have their grandchildren experience a revival, also. May such grandparents make it their passion to be a catalyst for a revival their grandchildren will experience—to pass the torch of revival to them. In every church, let the cry of compassion from grandparents for the grandchildren they love impel them to cry out to God for His sweeping and ongoing move.

An unrevived church turns inward to its own concerns, to established religion, to oiling the religious machinery, to caring for itself, to enlarging its congregation, to enlarging its building. A revived church—rooted certainly in loving, inward fellowship—turns outward to speak to its world, to encounter it and its sins wherever it is, and to minister to the nation.

Real revivals shake and change society and individuals. In a revival, public and private sin is confronted and repentance demanded. This is one of the untapped and potentially most productive means of evangelism.

Early in our *Cry of the Innocents* ministry, my wife and I had questions about what the Lord seemed to be opening to us. It all had opened so incredibly—we still find it amazing—but I had questions. Is what is opening appropriate? Is it correct to be speaking about "an issue" such as abortion? I had spoken in Europe and was being invited to other places in the world. I had seen positive responses. Yet inwardly I wondered about it all and asked the Lord for direction and wisdom.

Then, while on one of my first speaking itineraries, a three-week schedule arranged by a Christian organization, the Lord wonderfully began to unfold His answer. In one speaking engagement something very remarkable happened. Now I am very careful about drawing inferences from personal experiences because they can be misunderstood and misused, but I'm certain I've done neither. The engagement was a public meeting on a Tuesday night—about 200 people attended. Close to one-fourth were Catholic, the others were Protestant from various denominations: Methodist, Episcopal, Assembly of God, etc. I spoke the same as I had all along the tour, but as I look back I can see that on that evening there was a special anointing.

I came to the end of my address and then said something that I now find incredible. I told the audience that we came from various church backgrounds, but if they would like to pray for the country, why not make the chair ahead of them a place of prayer. The moment I said that, there was an exceptional response. Nearly the whole audience went to their knees and began to weep. The scene so amazed me that I didn't know how to respond—I was stunned. It was as if something I had read about in church history was happening right before my eyes.

Then, still not knowing what was happening or what to say, I said, "Perhaps we could have different ones lead out in short prayers, one after another." Immediately people began to pray, weeping as they did. They prayed openly in repentance of both personal and public sin, some even openly confessed abortion and pornography. With tears pouring down their faces and sobs punctuating their prayers, they asked the Lord to send a mighty revival to their city. On and on it went. People of all denominations melted together, broken before the Lord by the power of the Holy Spirit. He was powerfully present.

I was so overwhelmed that during the praying I knelt and put my face into the carpet and broke into tears. Then the Lord began to answer my questions about what I was doing by instructing me from the Scriptures. To my mind came an exposition of the second chapter of Acts that I had given some months before. I don't remember where the outline for the exposition came from, whether it was from something I had read or if it just opened to me at the time, but there were four things from Acts 2 that stood out, four things that seemed to form a pattern for the kind of Church the Lord would use, a Church whose voice would be the prophetic voice that is needed today. The fourth thing, I remember, was specifically helpful to explain the purpose of the ministry opening to me and why speaking out on public sins such as killing our unborn could be powerfully strategic.

Other insights about the prospect of this ministry unfolded to me that night while I was on my face before God and in the days just after—insights that have developed wondrously since. In fact, the seeds of this book—particularly this chapter and the next—were planted that evening.

Churches God Will Use

What the Holy Spirit opened to me through the Scriptures, in the beauty of that singular meeting, was that the Lord would give a sweeping harvest, and the kind of revival that shakes and changes society, to those local churches and parishes who prayerfully and humbly committed themselves to be the kind of fellowships He could entrust with such a move.

God was looking for local churches and parishes of *character*—the place where spiritual warfare begins—to be the channel of the Holy Spirit and revival power. In such charactered churches, there would be four key essentials found in Acts 2.

Acts 2 tells what occurred on the Day of Pentecost in the first days and weeks of the Church. If we asked almost any pastor or church leader if they would like to see happening today what is recorded in Acts 2:41, they would probably answer with a strong, "Yes!" Read what is written there: "Those who accepted his [Peter's] message were baptized, and about three thousand were added to their number that day."

What a harvest! What growth! Yet the verse is the culmination of what happened earlier. Let's look at four things that are essential in a church that Christ would use.

The first essential is from Acts 2:1: "When the day of Pentecost came, they were all together in one place." The believers were in unity. On the Day of Pentecost, they had a bonded, committed fellowship. Their unity was such that "All the believers were one in heart and mind."[6] The record of their unity is inspiring and a model for any church that wishes to really have revival:

> They devoted themselves to the apostles' teaching and to the fellowship, to the breaking of bread and to prayer. Everyone was filled with awe, and many wonders and miraculous signs were done by the apostles. All the believers were together and had everything in common. Selling their possessions and goods, they gave to anyone as he had need. Every day they continued to meet together in the temple courts. They broke bread in their homes and ate together with glad and sincere hearts, praising God and enjoying the favor of all the people.[7]

The early Church had unity in prayer. Before the Day of Pentecost, they were in an upper room "joined together constantly in prayer."[8] Later, after the Day of

214

Pentecost, the believers faced persecution and "they raised their voices together in prayer to God."[9] Their prayer together no doubt helped develop their larger unity—partnering in prayer when there are challenges is a cement that bonds believers.

Our unity flows from the sacrifice of Christ: His broken body and shed blood is what we remember at the communion table. His body was broken so we could be whole, so we could be one body together. His blood was shed so we could be "blood relatives," one family.

There is dynamic power in such unity, more dynamic power than most of us comprehend. The miraculous flowed from the unity. Undeniably the enemy of our soul knows the power of such unity, and he will attack the Church's unity over and over. If he can stop our unity, he can stop the effectiveness of the Church. Satan might not really care how many miracle meetings we have, as long as when we are in our local church's prayer room, we are not in unity. Obtaining and maintaining unity is the greatest battle a local church or parish will have.

Jesus spoke of the awesome power of unity when He gave one of His most incredible—and authoritative—promises: "Again, I tell you that if two of you on earth agree about anything you ask for, it will be done for you by my Father in heaven."[10] Ask anything and it will be done by the Father. Amazing! But there must be agreement, there must be harmony, there must be two or more praying together as if playing a symphony. And that's hard to do. Jesus was not giving us some superficial formula to get our prayers answered—He was speaking of a deep, committed agreement that will bring the Father's response.

The context in which Jesus gave this promise in Matthew 18:19 concerns the steps to take when we have trouble with one another: "If your brother sins against you . . . ." The steps the Lord gives to resolve such times are meant to preserve unity. Sadly, local churches can be filled with sinning against one another—bickering, murmuring, gossiping, slandering—all the spirit of murder. For a church to have the agreement our Lord desires, let them repent of the sins of the spirit of murder. If a church expects to stand transparently before a world that has such a spirit of murder that it even kills its unborn, then repentance is essential. And when the church repents, let them turn toward one another in committed love.

The word the Lord uses in Matthew 18:19 for agreement speaks of a "symphony." A symphony, of course, is played by a large orchestra made up of diverse musical instruments, all brought together under one conductor, playing great music—if they are in harmony. In the diversity of the instruments, there is—can be—the unity that creates truly great music.

A local church has diverse kinds of people. Every congregation has those who are the melodious violin or sweet-flute types, as well as those who are the brassy horn or the loud-drum types. All are important; all are needed. But the Lord envisions the local church as a symphony, all in unity, all together. In a world of discord and jangle, the uplifting melody of loving unity from a church will be most attractive. Jesus said, "By this all men will know that you are my disciples, if you love one another."[11]

The symphony of a local church should activate fervent spiritual warfare. It should be the ongoing priority. After all, Jesus' promise is very clear: "If two of you on earth agree about anything you ask for, it will be done for you by my Father in heaven." Therefore, let the Church, for instance, agree on binding the powers of darkness and releasing the spirit of revival. Let it intercede in unity, and stand in the gap on behalf of the nation. Let the local church make unity their life-style.

The second essential: "All of them were filled with the Holy Spirit."[12] The believers were anointed. On that Day of Pentecost, the presence of the Holy Spirit was powerful, evidenced in the sound of the blowing of a violent wind, the tongues of fire, and the speaking in tongues.

Today, the work of the Holy Spirit is where many believers divide, which is sad, because we must have the anointing of the Holy Spirit to be effective. The reality, however, is that the doctrine of virtually every Christian denomination recognizes that it is only through the empowering of the Holy Spirit that Christians can accomplish what God desires. "Be filled with the Spirit,"[13] and "You will receive power when the Holy Spirit comes on you"[14] are Scripture statements Christians should agree on. The anointing of the Holy Spirit is not just a goal, but a gate—not just an experience, but a life-style.

Cherishing God's Presence

The presence of the Holy Spirit—the very presence of God—is what every believer and every church or parish should cherish. We are to live in His presence. And the moment we sense we have grieved the Holy Spirit, the moment we are aware His beautiful presence is not evident, we should stop everything and run to the Lord in repentance—because we must have the Holy Spirit's presence; we cannot live without Him. His continuous presence is what the early Church had[15] and what we so terribly lack.

Sadly, today we can operate our churches too easily without the Holy Spirit. We know how to practice church, and we have much established religion that does not need to depend on the anointing of the Holy Spirit; indeed, depending on the Holy Spirit is often the last thing on our minds. We are too often like Samson who did not realize that the Spirit had departed when he tried to fight the Philistines. But the resulting sterile religion, as in Amos's day, is the enemy of society—it dulls the conscience of a society that is heading toward judgment.

May our churches recover their awareness of God's glory, yearn for it, cry for it, obtain it, maintain it, and absolutely depend on it. It makes little sense for preachers and churches to rail at the world about their sins unless the glory of God is in the midst of the Church—for in that glory is the power of conviction, and therein lies the only hope for change.

So, in whatever part of the religious spectrum our denomination belongs—evangelical, charismatic, reformed, Pentecostal, Catholic—we must have in our churches a deep hunger and an impelling thirst for the life of the Holy Spirit. He is indispensable. We must realize that without Him, we have only an empty and false ministry. Let our hearts be set to behold, as Isaiah did, the very glory of the holy God, and then to realize our great need and the need of the world and repent. It is then that our lips will be touched by the cleansing fire of the Holy Spirit. This is the kind of church that God can use today. Let the local church make the anointing of the Holy Spirit their heart-cry.

The third essential: "Men of Israel, listen to this: Jesus of Nazareth was a man accredited by God to you."[16] The believers were Christ-focused. On that Day of Pentecost, when the crowd had gathered after the believers had been filled with the Holy Spirit, Peter stood and preached. Peter explained what was happening from the prediction of Joel and said, "And everyone who calls on the name of the Lord will be saved."[17] Then Peter boldly proclaimed Christ as Messiah, Savior, and risen Lord. Peter used the Word of God to lift up Christ. His focus was on Christ: Christ had done miracles, Christ had been killed by them,

Christ had been buried, Christ had arisen, Christ was at the right hand of God, Christ had poured out the Holy Spirit.

Our focus must be on Christ. He redeemed us, He shed His blood for us, He is the answer to the world's sin, He is the only way to the Father—no other name will save.

Every church or parish should toughly evaluate its ministries—men's, women's, youth, children's, Sunday morning, whatever—to see what is emphasized, what is being taught, and whether people are maturing in Christ, knowing God, understanding redemption, growing in grace. It should be a growing church through growing people. Each pastor should firmly examine what he is preaching, what he is saying, what he is leaving out, whom he is trying to please and why. He should examine whether his ministry has false elements about and whether he will warn the people. Israel and Judah's idolatry and great sin were because the people did not know God. God placed the blame for this lack of knowledge on the priests and the prophets, those who were entrusted to teach His Word. So we *must* proclaim Christ. Proclaiming Christ is more than a clever slogan; it involves the whole counsel of God and the whole character of God from the entire Word of God.

Let the local church make focusing on Christ their vision.

These three, then—being united, anointed, and Christ-focused—are essentials that build that strong character in a local church that will make them spiritually effective in revival—and make essential number four effectual.

Churches and parishes like that will have the character God demands. They will be a disciplined, humble, repentant people who want truth, not fads, and who deeply care for one another. They will have a heart after God, know His grief over sin, and take the warnings of the Scriptures seriously. They will understand their special opportunity in a defining moment like today and will not be diverted through worldliness and the deceptions of today's false, destructive philosophies. Rather, they will see the world through the eyes of Christ, and motivated by His love, they will take up their cross and stand for Him in the world.

Readied for the Fourth Essential

Of the four essentials in Acts 2, the first three are pastoral concerns. It is my view that the Church is struggling between these first three and number four—the prophetic voice, which we discuss in detail in the next chapter. Some of our wrestling today over whether to speak up on "issues" or to get involved in politics or speak in public could be part of the struggle we seem to go through when the Lord nudges us on to enlarged ministry. To be effective, however, a church should not attempt essential number four without focusing first on one, two, and three. Many churches and groups attempt number four, but are ineffective in the way God really wants them to be used, because they leave out the first three. They rush out, flail about, say the right things, say the wrong things, and are not productive—not in the New Testament sense, at least. The reason is that their zeal has no roots.

There is the opposite danger—perhaps the more evident one today—and that is that churches focus on one, two, and three, but stop short of number four and never step forward, not quite sure they should. So their focus turns inward.

God wants to release revival. He wants to make His Church a prophetic voice. He wants ministry to the nation. To accomplish this, He focuses on the character and integrity of those He uses. He wants to develop the kind of people who can be trusted with the move of His Holy Spirit. Such a people will want to know Him and His love, the message of the cross, and live in the power of Christ's resurrection. They will look beyond the narrow "now" by having the larger look of eternity and will bring that enlarged look to their message. Personal holiness and a heart after God will be their focus.

These will be evident in a vibrant, united, anointed, Christ-focused congregation. These first three essentials are vital, imperative. Let every church major on them! Let every pastor, elder, deacon—the keys—lead their local fellowship to these three. Let them nurture these characteristics, place them as the priority, and guard against diversion from them.

Such a church will have a dynamic and uplifting attitude, will vigorously engage in spiritual warfare, will have a toughness that today demands, will have a vision to move ahead in Christ, and will have an over-arching passion to let nothing hold them back from raising God's cry of compassion in the world!

---

[1] Isaiah 60:1-3.

[2] Paul Lowenberg, sermon, "The Mandate of the Church" given at Assemblies of God Council on Evangelism, 1968.

[3] Ibid.

[4] Richard Halverson, interview in *Christianity Today*, (November 12, 1982).

[5] Jack Hayford, *Above and Beyond*, (Living Way Ministries, Van Nuys, CA, 1986), pp. 13-14.

[6] Acts 4:32.

[7] Acts 2:42-47.

[8] Acts 1:14.

[9] Acts 4:24.

[10] Matthew 18:19.

[11] John 13:35.

[12] Acts 2:4.
[13] Ephesians 5:18.
[14] Acts 1:8.
[15] Acts 15:28.
[16] Acts 2:22.
[17] Acts 2:21.

15

The Prophetic Voice

Now, when our land to ruin's brink is verging.
In God's name let us speak while there is time:
Now, when the padlocks for our lips are forging,
Silence is a crime.

John Greenleaf Whittier

I heard a minister tell of once driving alone, late at night, along a lonely stretch of road. He was sleepy, but was jolted wide awake as his headlights picked up the form of a man standing on the road, waving his arms. The minister slowed, but steered the car to go around the man. But the man quickly moved in front of his car, waving frantically. He looked unsavory, disheveled, dirty, and appeared to be bleeding. Apprehensive, the minister didn't want to stop, so he again steered the car to get around the man. And again the man moved quickly in front of the car, extremely agitated. The minister, now going very slow, carefully rolled his window down and stuck his head out. The man yelled at him, "Stop, stop! The bridge is out, the bridge is out!"

A torrent of water from a recent storm had

collapsed a bridge just ahead, and the man had driven his car off the bridge into the river. He had miraculously survived, crawled out of his demolished automobile, and gotten back up onto the roadway to warn other drivers.

The minister said: "I'm very glad that man kept getting in my way, got frantic, and yelled at me! He may have saved my life."

Genuine prophets are like that. Prophetic voices are urgent, even frantic, in their manner—and we can be thankful they are. Like Amos or John the Baptist, when we are in spiritual danger—and asleep to our peril—they get in our way and stay there. They forcefully confront us and press God's message to us so we will forsake our compromised lives, repent, and come to Him.

Today we need to hear from those with such bold voices. We need them to face us straight on, call us to confront our sins, warn us of judgment, and command us to repent. However, we in the Church can get edgy with urgent people and insist on silencing anyone raising their voice. Sadly, many times we are more concerned with proper manners, good "PR," and congenial personality than the moral sewer rising around us.

This is prime time for the Church! It is time for the Church to speak to America, the nation "under God" who professes to trust in God but who has rejected God, and declare firmly as Amos did: "Prepare to meet your God." The Church's bold, biblical proclamation of God's Word will be pivotal in today's spiritual warfare, in bringing down the powers of darkness, and in bringing men and women to Christ. It could be a catalyst for revival. But *the Church must speak.* Its prophetic voice must be raised. Our dilemma is acute. Judgment looms.

The prophetic voice of the Church must clearly

"preach the Word"[1] to the situation today. The Word of God stands in judgment over every modern philosophy and mind set. God is speaking to us about our society and nation, but we must hear His Word to perceive it.

The prophetic cry must come from those who know God, who know His heart, and who have a passion after Him. It must arise out of hearts of compassion and it must come from churches in which there is unity, anointing, and focus on Christ.

As we saw in the last chapter, the Lord will only use churches of character, and He to wants to develop their character so that He can use them. We examined three essentials in that character; now let's examine the fourth. We will look at Peter's sermon on that Day of Pentecost—when Peter "preached the Word"—and examine what happened and what we can learn from it.

The fourth essential comes from Acts 2:40: "With many other words he warned them; and he pleaded with them, 'Save yourselves from this corrupt generation.'" Peter became prophetic, and here we see another part of spiritual warfare: bold, biblical preaching.

At the beginning and conclusion of his Christ-focused sermon, Peter pointedly charged the crowd with the death of Christ: "You, with the help of wicked men, put him to death.[2]. . . this Jesus, whom you crucified."[3] These statements took courage. Peter boldly NAMED THEIR SIN, which was the shedding of the most innocent blood ever shed, the sinless blood of Jesus Christ. Peter was direct about their sin, he used the word "you"—*you did it!*

The impact was powerful: "When the people heard this, they were cut to the heart"—stabbed in their consciences and convicted of their sin. To awaken them to their spiritual need, to their dark and lost condition, they needed to be penetrated to the center of their being. The crowd was predominantly religious and

225

most of them were there for Pentecost, so they had little sense of sin. But seven weeks before, many in this same crowd had participated in the murder of Jesus, and most of them had heard of Him and rejected Him as God's "Anointed One" and Son.

Today our society is primarily secular with little sense of sin and needs to be cut to the heart over its iniquity. The language of sin must be used to address the people, and they must be made to realize the certainty that their choices have consequences—that there is judgment for the choices they have made. More than any new social program or economic stimulus or political change, America and the West must be cut to the heart by the prophetic Word of God.

John Wesley, who believed in "speaking of death and judgment, heaven and hell," as George Catlin said of him, "to arouse men to consciousness of their actual, present, damnation-deserving sin," wrote of the effect of his preaching at a factory:

> A large number . . . were employed. The whole conversation of these was profane and loose to the last degree. But some of them stumbling in at the prayer meeting were suddenly cut to the heart. These never rested until they had gained their companions. The whole scene changed . . . . No more lewdness or profaneness were found; for God had put a new song in their mouth, and blasphemies were turned to praise."[4]

For Peter to have gone against the Holy Spirit's anointing and soothed the crowd with a "peace, peace" message, and not awakened them to their sin, would have been lamentable, a breach of his message. For him to have stood there and replaced God's wisdom with his own and preached some currently favorite Gospel fad, and omitting mention of their sin, would have been a flagrant betrayal of what the Lord had placed him there to do. Without question, the powerful response would not have happened. They would not have confessed their sin and forsaken their wickedness. Peter would have been a false prophet.

How many times have we not seen a Day of Pentecost response because we have shaded and shaped God's Word to avoid the hard truth? Hard truth is still truth. This is no call for harshness, but a call for integrity in keeping with the mandate of the Gospel.

But Peter had his message right, and the crowd desperately cried to him and the other apostles, "What shall we do?" Peter went to the point, "Repent and be baptized, every one of you, in the name of Jesus Christ for the forgiveness of your sins." Under the Spirit's anointing, Peter preached a long sermon: "With many other words he warned them; and he pleaded with them." Though a lengthy discourse, Peter's topic was focused: "Save yourselves from this corrupt generation."[5]

Peter candidly described society as "this corrupt generation," which is God's view of our fallen world. The generation was corrupt—a moral and spiritual sewer, depraved, debauched, completely sinful. Morals, religious activity, entertainment, music, sports, business, politics—whatever sinful man had touched— were affected. But let us note that Peter, directed by the Spirit, DIDN'T PUT A BETTER FACE ON THE WORLD THAN GOD DOES. He called it "corrupt."

What about today? Are we corrupt? Look at our hands with the blood of unborn innocents on them, look at our streets unsafe with violence and crime, look at our public attitudes with the vilest sexual perversions accepted, look at us with deserved judgment looming, look at us like Sodom: "arrogant, overfed, unconcerned." We are no different. Are we honest with God's Word, and are we honest with our hearers when we so readily put a better face on our world than Peter did on his and we preach "peace-peace" themes? If we do, we will have to answer to God, because our world's problems are much more than a bad self-image.

Peter's message was urgent; he commanded them to get out of this evil world. "Save yourselves from . . . ," he proclaimed, meaning, "Get out! Leave! Forsake this debauched world's evil. Hey! I'm speaking to YOU." Implicit in Peter's call was the command to repent and come to Christ. His passion was like the angels trying to get Lot and his family out of Sodom before the imminent devastation: "Flee for your lives!" the angels said.[6] It's imperative. Do it now or you'll be destroyed. Does it bother us to have someone speak so strongly? Desperate times call for strong words. We need them now. Our world is corrupt and the unsaved must be told to flee from it and run to Christ.

Peter did two other things: first, "HE WARNED THEM." Warning speaks of clarity and completeness. Peter gave no partial, selected message—there was a warning in it. Faithfulness to the Word of God insisted that they be warned. Peter was clear—sin brings judgment. If they continued in their sin, they would be judged. The crowd needed to be spiritually roused, and there is a roar in Peter's warning like the roar of the Lord as He spoke to sinning and slumbering Israel through Amos.[7]

Second, Peter "PLEADED WITH THEM." Here we come to the attitude that motivated Peter. Pleading speaks of compassion and caring. The heart of Peter was moved with love for those to whom he spoke. Compassion impelled him to raise his voice in warning, to call the crowd to get out of this corrupt world—he MUST speak; love demanded that he speak.

Peter had seen compassion. He was there when Jesus saw crowds "harassed and helpless, like sheep without a shepherd"[8] and was moved by compassion.

Peter was there when Jesus wept at Lazarus' grave, and when He wept over Jerusalem. Peter had watched Jesus touch the sick and comfort children.

But more than that, Peter had experienced compassion—personally—just a few weeks before on the shore of Galilee. Peter, who had betrayed the Lord and wept bitterly in despair, had met Jesus with other disciples after a night of fishing. Jesus had lovingly restored Peter by asking him three times the searching question, "Do you truly love me?"

Peter knew God's love. It was this Peter who pled with the crowd. Yes, his words were strong; yes, his voice was raised; yes, he spoke of sin; yes, he warned. But he was motivated by the compassion of honest love to say the things he did.

Through Peter, the crowd heard something that every crowd, every individual, needs to hear every time a man or woman of God speaks: THEY HEARD THE HEART OF GOD. They heard the cry of the Father, THE CRY OF COMPASSION that expressed our Lord's grief over sin and His concern for humanity as nothing else could.

Peter's sermon had the two essential elements needed to bind up the wounds of sin: (1) the needle, (2) the thread. The needle is God's Law, His commandments. The thread is the Gospel of Jesus Christ, God's grace. To suture a wound, both a needle and thread are needed, they are indispensable to one another. If only the needle is used, the wound is made worse. If only the thread is used, the wound is not bound up. When both are used, however, they draw together the wound so that it can heal. Both are essential, one is no good without the other. Let's preach the full Word of God, using the Law of God as the necessary needle to draw along the binding thread of the Gospel.

We should not be afraid to use the Law in our

preaching; it is not our enemy. In the Scriptures, the Law came before grace came. It is God's sequence, and we cannot improve upon it. If there is no law, there is no grace. The purpose of the Law is to show us our need for Christ. If we are not irrevocably convicted of our sins by the Law, then we will never feel a need for Christ. To use a dull needle or wave a limp thread at people in the name of biblical preaching in our falling society is both a travesty and dishonest, plus it is not true compassion. Most critical, however, is that it doesn't heal spiritual wounds, and we could wind up with a congenial crowd of people in our meetings who say, "Lord, Lord," but are not doing the will of the Father and will therefore perish in eternal judgment.[9] This is often happening today.

On the Day of Pentecost, Peter preached the Word of God, clearly, faithfully, with warnings, with compassion. What was the result of this biblical preaching? The response was stunning: "THOSE WHO ACCEPTED HIS MESSAGE WERE BAPTIZED, AND ABOUT THREE THOUSAND WERE ADDED TO THEIR NUMBER THAT DAY"[10] (Emphasis mine). When we listen to Peter, there is something about his words and tone that sound familiar. His theme, "Save yourselves from this corrupt generation," sounds like something we have heard others say. Who? Where?

It sounds like the prophets. It is certainly something that Jeremiah could have said, or Hosea, or Zephaniah, or John the Baptist. Jesus assuredly could have said it. They all said things like it. Peter had the voice of the prophet. This is the *fourth essential* that our Lord wants in His Church today: A PROPHETIC VOICE.

The Apostle Peter stood with united, anointed, Christ-focused believers behind him and boldly proclaimed God's Word to the crowd before him. Peter and the Church stood face to face with the world, and in the power of the Holy Spirit[11] backed the people up against a spiritual wall until they cried, "What must we do to be saved?" A mighty spiritual move had started. The early Church paid a great price for it—they were persecuted, some were martyred, but the Church of Christ marched forward undaunted. With the help and power of that same Spirit that anointed Peter, it is now time for another Day of Pentecost proclamation.

There are things that only the Church can do, and if it does not do them, they will not get done. Intercessory prayer and preaching the Word of God—both part of a prophetic voice—are two of them. For these, we are stewards. If the Church does not raise a prophetic voice, it will not be raised—not from legislatures, parliaments, or social agencies. It will, and can, only come from the Church.

The Church must start being the Church, doing what only the Church can do. We live in a defining time, defined by our sins, and with our sins determining our future. The signs of our decline are evident and, if ignored, point only to our destruction. And ignoring them we are.

As we in the Church do what only the Church can do, we'll increasingly face a hostile world with an attitude like that of Pilate. With Jesus on trial before him, Pilate made a virtue out of moral neutrality. He ceremonially washed his hands in a basin of water and pronounced, "I am innocent of this man's blood."[12] With that, Jesus was sent to His death. Today, from abortion to immorality, moral fence-sitting rules—and we presumptuously believe that such a position absolves us of accountability.

Today we wash our hands over a basin of self-professed pro-choice neutrality and allow millions of unborn to go to their deaths in the womb, arrogantly believing we are not responsible. We've convinced ourselves that shedding innocent blood is acceptable, and we allow the killing to go on unchecked—and,

231

worse, unchallenged—because our conscience has become numb to our ongoing crime.

But Pilate was not absolved of accountability, and neither are we. No posturing over basins of water absolves anyone—nation or individual—from responsibility for the killing of innocent human beings. We have blood on our hands and basin-washing doesn't remove it. Neutrality is no defense, and we are not going to be able to stand before God and plead "pro-choice" as an alibi as to why we stood on the sidelines and permitted a holocaust against the unborn. We stand answerable to God, and now our guilt is piling up like water rising behind a dam, ready to be released in our hour of judgment.

Our society is also like Judas. Judas betrayed Jesus. He gained a personal benefit of thirty pieces of silver. For personal benefit, we have betrayed our unborn. For our personal convenience, we have killed millions of them. Will the day come when, like Judas, we're shaken awake to what we have done, when the weight of what we've permitted jolts our conscience, and seized with remorse, we cry, "I [we] have sinned, for I [we] have betrayed innocent blood"?[13]

Will we then, like Judas, despise our "thirty pieces of silver," our blood money? Judas killed himself. His judgment was at his own hands. Ours is at the hands of God.

We need a prophetic voice, one like Elijah's. Elijah preached in a fence-sitting time when the nation tried to serve God *and* Baal. The nation was sinning. At one crucial juncture in Israel, Elijah confronted the king, the nation, and the prophets of Baal with the challenge: "How long will you waver between two opinions? If the Lord is God, follow him; but if Baal is God, follow him."[14] Elijah sharply defined the issue.

The test was whether Baal or God would answer by fire—a fair test. Baal sent no fire, but God did. The people fell prostrate and cried, "The Lord—he is God!"[15] Picture Elijah today thundering into our society where only the names of the idolatries are different, but the double-mindedness and decadence are the same. Elijah stands before the morally ambivalent pastors and preachers, the political leaders and educators, the lawyers and doctors, the parents and public, and cries out, "How long will you waver between two opinions? If the LORD is God, follow him; but if Baal is God, follow him!" What would the answer be in our nation today?

May the Church raise such a challenge. Our cup of iniquity is getting full, things are being shaken, the bloodshed of innocents and gross perversion pollute our land, and we are reaping the wreckage from our sinful choices. We stand at the bar of God; and He has heard the cry of our aborted unborn; and, as He did at Sodom, He has come down among us to "see if what they have done is as bad as the outcry that has reached me." When the Lord told Abraham about Sodom's coming judgment, he interceded before the Lord.[16] Let us do so now. And let us call our world to repentance—knowing that our only safety now is the safety of repentance.

The late Peter Marshall, once Chaplain of the United States Senate, preached a sermon on Elijah's confrontation on Mount Carmel. Marshall spoke to the materialistic attitudes that had arisen in the nation, contrasted materialism with the worship of God, and spoke of the need for a revival. He concluded his sermon in a riveting way. Marshall issued Elijah's challenge to the congregation, and to America, and concluded with the statement: "If God is God, serve Him. But if Baal is God, serve him . . . and go to hell!"

In the spirit of Elijah, it is time for a modern Mount Carmel. This brings us again to a question asked in the first chapter of this book: *Has America gone too far?* There came such a time in Israel, Judah, and the pagan nations—a time when God determined to judge them.

Why not us? Why do we arrogantly persist in the self-serving idea that we can escape judgment? I say again, every day that America—or any nation in the West—does not repent, only confirms America's rebellion against God and increases this nation's condemnation—and hastens its judgment.

As the days pass, America is running out of time! At some point, we may be jolted to find out that contrasted with the holy and compassionate God of Scripture who loved us and sent His Son to be our Savior, the amicable, congenial "god" we have become so adept at presenting is, in fact, an idol of our own making, and we are idolaters, and we face His judgment

Derek Prince, in his foreword for this book, put our situation this way: "I feel that these judgments are closer at hand than most of us are willing to recognize, and that God may not prove to be so 'nice' as many contemporary preachers depict Him."

Can there be revival? Perhaps, if we in the Church seek the Lord, but WE ARE RUNNING OUT OF TIME, and every day the Church remains distracted only hastens the nation's judgment. Every careless, luke-warm church is the best-friend of the nation's sin; each cold, worldly church speeds the nation's collapse; each one is the ally of national iniquity, offering nothing to stop moral rot, its prophetic voice silenced. If there is to be revival, the Church must repent; we must start giving altar calls to professed Christians.

Can there be revival with judgment looming? Again, perhaps; but we must seek the Lord WITHOUT DELAY! Nineveh had only "forty days" before judgment, Jonah's message from God said. But as we have seen, Nineveh deeply repented, from king to peasant, and God relented even at that late hour from sending the judgment. God was "a gracious and compassionate God, slow to anger and abounding in love, a God who relents from sending calamity."[17]

However, we must stress that the hour is late for us. What saved Nineveh was the preaching of God's Word by Jonah at the late hour; and they repented.

Every day they did not have the preaching of Jonah, every day they did not repent, only moved them inexorably toward their judgment.

The question is: Where are our Jonahs? We can only take encouragement from Nineveh if Jonah's words are being preached and we are repenting. America must now hear a "forty days and you will be destroyed" message, because the days toward our judgment are counting off for us.

Will there be national revival? God knows. But what would happen if like Nineveh, from our leaders—president, prime minister, cabinet, leading officials, and members of the Senate and House of Representatives—all the way to the man or woman in the street, to you and I, repented? What might God do?

We do believe we are to seek the Lord, and that He hears—and answers—those who seek Him. We do believe local churches seeking the Lord can have revival—and local areas.

The response of our nation—and any in the West—may be like a story that was told to me several years ago, a story like the one which began this chapter. I was in the Australian city of Hobart, Tasmania, on a speaking itinerary and was riding in an automobile driven by a friend. As we approached the long, arching harbor bridge, my friend recalled the time years before when a large ship had accidently rammed and knocked out one of the bridge's huge center pillars, bringing down a whole section. Speeding automobiles, he said, began plunging into the abyss; but one car came to a stop right on the edge. The driver carefully climbed out and ran back down the bridge to warn others. How-ever, to his horror, as he waved frantically and shouted warnings, drivers ignored him and sped on to disaster. He kept it up, and eventually traffic was stopped.

Can our drive toward disaster be stopped? Can there be revival? Let us raise our voice boldly to a prophetic voice! May that raised voice be a CRY OF COMPASSION, motivated by the heart of the Father. And may we raise that voice in bold prayer and bold proclamation—two primary weapons in spiritual warfare. May we get on our knees in the private place of prayer and raise a cry of compassionate intercession on behalf of our world for a spiritual awakening, leading the way in repentance; and then may we stand on our feet in the public arena and pulpit and raise the cry of compassionate proclamation of the Word of God, declaring such calls as, "Save yourselves from this corrupt generation!"

May our cry today be A COMPASSIONATE ROAR! And may it be heard from the pulpit of every church and parish. Urgency demands it. David McKenna says, "The time is come for the prophetic voice of evangelical Christians to be heard, locally and nationally, in the immediate present."[18]

We are in that time our Lord spoke of, the time as in the days of Noah and Sodom.[19] We await His glorious return. Tragically, however, it's business-as-usual while our sins are exceedingly great and our land is filled with bloodshed and perversion. Our land needs to be healed.

God begins with His people, with you, with me. It is time now for judgment to begin at the house of God. So let us look again at our Lord's counsel:

> If my people, who are called by my name, will humble themselves and pray and seek my face and turn from their wicked ways, then I will hear from heaven and will forgive their sin AND WILL HEAL THEIR LAND[20] (Emphasis mine).

May what this Scripture, and others like it, call us to do now be our national priority.

We need a national prayer meeting. Now. For repentance. For turning to the Lord. And such a prayer meeting must be in every church and parish; it needs to be at the top of our agenda. May the Church raise a needed prophetic voice and call us to this. It will be the most compassionate thing the Church will now do.

At this defining time, THERE IS ULTIMATELY NO OTHER QUESTION BEFORE US. Not economic. Not political. Not social.

And with John Hampden Gurney (1802-62), may we pray:

> With one consent we meekly bow
>> beneath Thy chastening hand
> And pouring forth confession meet,
>> mourn with our mourning land;
> With pitying eye behold our need
>> as thus we lift our prayer
> *Correct us with Thy judgments, Lord,*
>> *then let Thy mercy spare.*
>
> (Emphasis mine)

---

[1] 2 Timothy 4:2.

[2] Acts 2:23.

[3] Acts 2:36.

[4] George Catlin, *The Anglo-Saxon Tradition*, (Broadway House, London, 1939), p. 191.

[5] Acts 2:37-40.

[6] Genesis 19:17.

[7] Amos 1:2.

[8] Matthew 9:36.

[9] Matthew 7:21, 22.

[10] Acts 2:41.

[11] Acts 1:8.

[12] Matthew 27:24.

[13] Matthew 27:4.

[14] 1 Kings 18:21.

[15] 1 Kings 18:39.

[16] Genesis 18:22-33.

[17] Jonah 4:2.

[18] David I. McKenna, "A Pure Note Above the Noise," (*United Evangelical Action*, Winter, 1982).

[19] Luke 17:26-28.

[20] 2 Chronicles 7:14.